THE OFFICIAL DRIVER'S HANDBOOK

TRAFFIC LAWS AND GOOD DRIVING PRACTICES FOR DRIVERS IN ONTARIO

This booklet is a guide only. For official purposes, please refer to the Highway Traffic Act, the Motorized Snow Vehicles Act and the Off-Road Vehicles Act of Ontario.

Disponible en français
Demandez le «Guide officiel de l'automobiliste»

Driving is a privilege—not a right

THE OFFICIAL DRIVER'S HANDBOOK

Introduction

Ontario's goal is to make its roads the safest in North America, and that's why the Ministry of Transportation has introduced a range of measures to improve the behaviour of all drivers, including new ones.

Every year, more than 1,100 people are killed and 90,000 are injured on Ontario roads. The social and economic costs of these collisions are estimated at $9 billion annually.

Most collisions—85 per cent—are caused by driver error—behaviour like drinking and driving, careless driving and driving too fast. And statistics show that new drivers of all ages are far more likely than experienced drivers to be involved in serious or fatal collisions.

Ontario campaigns against drinking and driving, aggressive driving and promoting the correct use of seat belts and child safety seats are making a difference. Graduated licensing, which lets new drivers gain skills and experience in low-risk environments, is also helping to develop better, safer drivers.

This handbook gives new drivers the basic information they need about learning to drive in Ontario: the rules of the road, safe driving practices and how to get their licence to drive a car, van or small truck.

As you read, remember that this is only a guide. For more detailed information about driving you can read the book Road Worthy, a driving textbook produced by the Ministry of Transportation. For official descriptions of the laws, look in the Highway Traffic Act of Ontario and its Regulations.

Information on how to get licences to drive other types of vehicles is available in the Official Motorcycle Handbook, the Official Truck Handbook, the Official Bus Handbook, the Official Air Brake Handbook and the Official Off-Road Vehicles Handbook.

To find out how to get any of these publications, please see pages 132 and 139.

CONTENTS

CONTENTS

GETTING YOUR DRIVER'S LICENCE

This chapter tells you what licence you need to drive in Ontario and how to get it, whether you are a new driver, a visitor or a new resident in Ontario.

If you are applying for your first licence, this chapter explains the graduated licensing system, how to apply for a licence, the tests you will have to pass and the driving privileges you will have at each licence level.

What you need to drive in Ontario

If you live in Ontario, you must be at least 16 years old and have a valid Ontario driver's licence to drive in this province.

If you are a visitor to Ontario and want to drive while you are here, you must be at least 16 years old and have a valid driver's licence from your own province, state or country. If you are from another country and visiting Ontario for more than three months, you need an International Driver's Permit from your own country. If you don't have an International Driver's Permit, you can apply for an Ontario driver's licence.

If you are a new resident in Ontario and have a valid driver's licence from another province, state or country, you can use it for 60 days after you move to Ontario. If you want to keep driving in Ontario, you must get an Ontario driver's licence. Please see the section on new Ontario residents on page 13 for more information.

Quick Check Chart

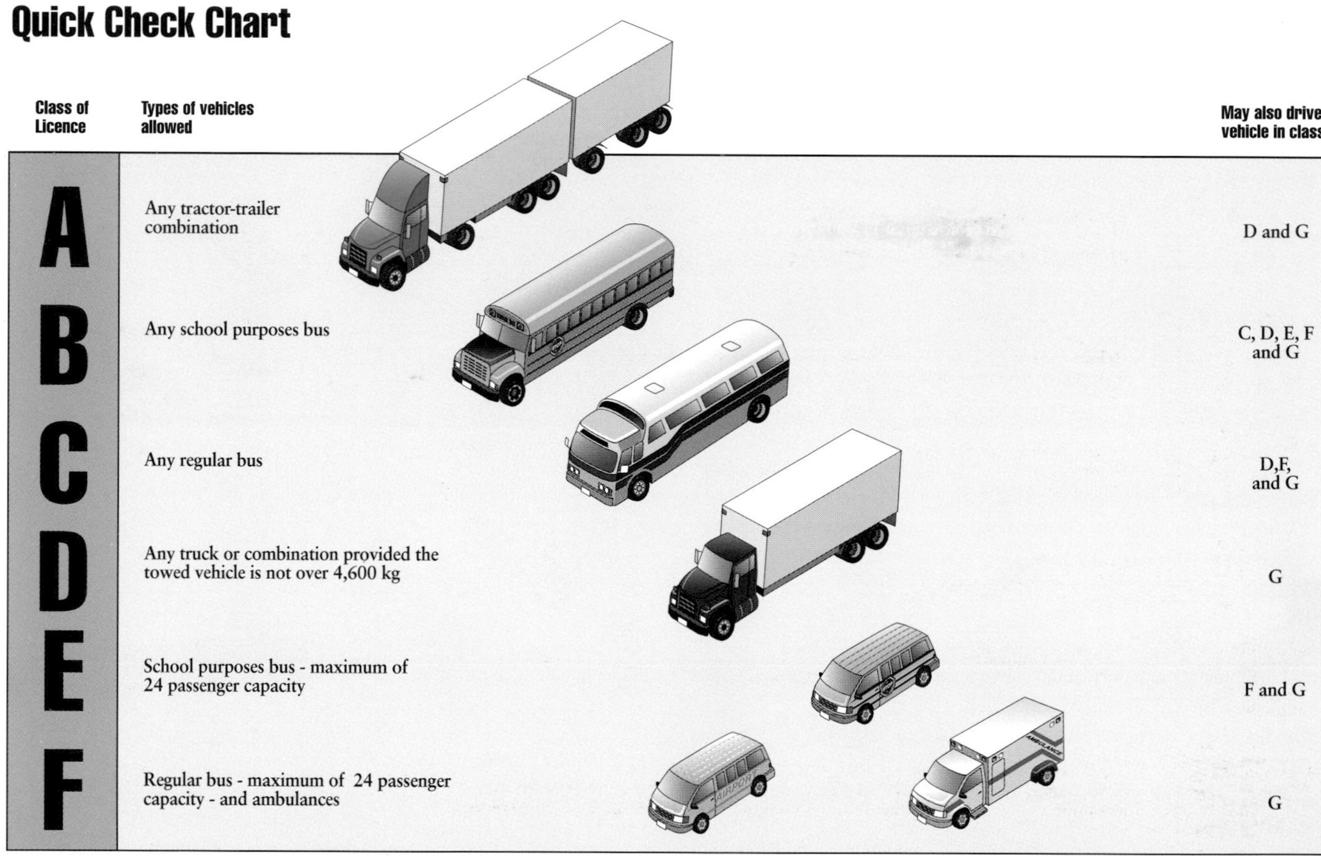

Class of Licence	Types of vehicles allowed	May also drive vehicle in class
A	Any tractor-trailer combination	D and G
B	Any school purposes bus	C, D, E, F and G
C	Any regular bus	D,F, and G
D	Any truck or combination provided the towed vehicle is not over 4,600 kg	G
E	School purposes bus - maximum of 24 passenger capacity	F and G
F	Regular bus - maximum of 24 passenger capacity - and ambulances	G

Diagram 1-1a

Class of Licence	Types of vehicles allowed	
G	Any car, van or small truck or combination of vehicle and towed vehicle up to 11,000 kg provided the towed vehicle is not over 4,600 kg   	
G1	Level One of graduated licensing Holders may drive Class G vehicles when accompanied by a fully licensed driver with at least four years of driving experience. Additional conditions apply.	REPLACES CLASS L LICENCE
G2	Level Two of graduated licensing Holders may drive Class G vehicles without accompanying driver but are subject to certain conditions.	REPLACES PROBATIONARY STATUS
M	Motorcycles Holders may also drive a Class G vehicle under the conditions that apply to a Class G1 licence holder. 	
M1	Level One of graduated licensing. Holders may drive a motorcycle under certain conditions.	REPLACES CLASS R LICENCE
M2	Level Two of graduated licensing Holders may drive a motorcycle but only with a zero blood alcohol level. Holders may also drive a Class G vehicle under the conditions that apply to a Class G1 licence holder.	REPLACES PROBATIONARY STATUS

Diagram 1-1b A "Z" air brake endorsement is required on a driver's licence to operate any air brake equipped motor vehicles.

Getting your driver's licence

What kind of licence?

In Ontario, there are 12 different kinds of licences. Each one qualifies you to drive a different type of vehicle. The class of licence you have must match the type of vehicle you are driving. You need a Class G licence to drive a car, van or small truck. You must have a Class G licence before you can be licensed to drive any other type of vehicle. The only exception is motorcycles. You may get a motorcycle licence (Class M) without first getting a Class G licence. The Quick Check Chart on page 6 shows you what class of licence you need to drive different vehicles.

For information on the skills and knowledge you'll need to get a Class M motorcycle licence, study the Official Motorcycle Handbook.

You can get information on other kinds of licences — classes A,B,C,D,E and F — in the Official Truck Handbook and the Official Bus Handbook. If you want to drive a vehicle equipped with air brakes, the Official Air Brake Handbook tells you how to qualify.

Some recreational vehicles have special licence requirements. If you plan to drive an off-road vehicle, snowmobile or moped, or pull a trailer, you should read the Official Off-Road Vehicles Handbook.

You do not need a licence to ride a bicycle in Ontario.

Graduated licensing

As of April 1, 1994, new drivers applying for their first car or motorcycle licence enter Ontario's graduated licensing system. Graduated licensing lets new drivers get driving experience and skills gradually. The two-step licensing process takes at least 20 months to complete.

To apply for a licence, you must be at least 16 years old and pass a vision test and a test of your knowledge of the rules of the road and traffic signs. After you pass these tests, you will enter Level One and get a Class G1 licence and a novice driver information package. The package includes a sign you may want to hang in the rear window of the vehicle you use to practise driving. The 'N' sign lets other drivers know you are a new driver.

You must pass two road tests to become fully licensed. Passing the first road test lets you move to Level Two (Class G2) and the second one gives you full Class G driving privileges.

Probationary drivers

Before graduated licensing, newly licensed drivers were called probationary drivers and had to complete two 12-month probationary periods without having their licences suspended. The probationary driver system will continue until all new drivers licensed before April 1, 1994 complete their probationary periods.

Applying for a licence

To apply for a licence, you must show proof of your identity and the date of your birth. Documents must be original. The following documents are acceptable.

For date of birth and personal identification: (Must state day, month and year of birth)

- passport
- citizenship card
- Canada Immigration Form 1000 (record of landing)
- Permanent Resident Document (as of Fall 1994)
- photo driver's licence (expired or from another area)
- National Defence photo identification card
- Indian Treaty card
- certificate of Indian status
- deposition signed by the superintendent of a training school operated by Correctional Services
- sealed security identification which includes photo, signature and date of birth

For date of birth only: (Must state day, month and year of birth)

- birth certificate
- driver's licence (expired or from another area)
- baptismal certificate with official seal of church
- baptismal certificate, without seal, accompanied by other identification showing date of birth
- sworn affidavit with supporting documents

Getting your driver's licence

For personal identification only:
(Must bear applicant's signature)

- age of majority card
- Ontario Health card
- motor vehicle permit
- marriage certificate
- change of name certificate
- court order for name change
- certified adoption papers
- immigration card
- employee identification card
- student card
- credit card
- hospital card
- driver's licence photo (expired or from another area)
- membership card (such as library card, club membership)
- direct identification by a parent who has acceptable proof of identity and date of birth

Bring the documents to a Ministry of Transportation Driver Examination Centre or Travel Point (a temporary driver examination centre where there is no regional centre). Phone ahead to find out where the nearest Travel Point is and when it is open. You will find the number under Driver and Vehicle Licence Information in the Government of Ontario section of the blue pages in your phone book.

You must pay a fee when you apply. This fee includes the cost of the knowledge test and your first road test. There are more charges for your second road test and for any retests you may need to take.

When you apply for your licence, you will be asked questions about your health. People with some physical or medical conditions are not allowed to drive for safety reasons. If your physical or medical condition means you cannot be licensed, you will be told when you apply.

After you have a licence, you should report any change in your medical condition that may change your ability to drive safely. By law, doctors and optometrists must report the name and address of anyone over 16 who has a condition that may make it unsafe for him or her to drive.

Graduated licensing requirements
Here are the rules you must follow at each level:

Level One (Class G1):
Level One lasts 12 months. The Ministry of Transportation encourages all new drivers to take an approved driver education course to help learn the proper driving skills and knowledge. You should begin your training as soon as possible after becoming a Level One driver so you can get as much driving experience as

you can. If you pass an approved course, you can complete Level One in eight months. While at Level One:

- You must not drive if you have been drinking alcohol. Your blood alcohol level must be zero.
- You must not drive alone. A fully licensed driver with at least four years of driving experience must sit in the front passenger seat. This is the only person who can be in the front seat with you while you drive. Your accompanying driver must have a Class G or higher licence and a blood alcohol level of less than .05 per cent.
- Each person in the vehicle must have a working seat belt.
- You must not drive on 400-series roads with a posted speed limit over 80 km/h. Also, you must not drive on certain high-speed urban roads including the Queen Elizabeth Way, Don Valley Parkway and Gardiner Expressway in the Greater Toronto Area, the E.C. Row Expressway in Windsor and the Conestoga Parkway in Kitchener-Waterloo. However, if your accompanying driver is a driving instructor licensed in Ontario, you may drive on any road.
- You must not drive between midnight and 5 a.m.

You must pass a road test of your driving skills to move to Level Two. At this time, you will be given a Class G2 licence.

Level Two (Class G2):

Level Two lasts at least 12 months. At this level you have more privileges because of your driving experience. At Level Two:

- You must not drive if you have been drinking alcohol. Your blood alcohol level must be zero.
- Each person in the vehicle must have a working seat belt.

After 12 months at Level Two, you may take a road test to qualify for full licence privileges. You must pass this test to get a Class G licence.

Road tests

Road tests check your driving skills in the vehicle and in traffic. You will be tested on your ability to apply the rules of the road and safe driving practices.

The Level One road test deals with basic driving skills. The Level Two road test deals with more advanced knowledge and driving skills. Your performance in each of the tests will tell you whether you need more training or practice.

When you feel qualified to drive safely and confident enough to take your road test, contact a Ministry of Transportation Driver Examination Office or Travel Point to make an appointment. If you are unable to keep the appointment, phone the office immediately to cancel your test.

You must bring a vehicle for each of your road tests. Make sure it is a vehicle you are familiar with and is in good working order. Bring your current licence to the appointment. If you are a Level One driver, a fully licensed driver with at least four years of driving experience must come to the test centre with you.

During the road tests, no pets or passengers other than the driver examiner are allowed in the vehicle. The examiner may stop or refuse to start the driving test if:

- your vehicle is not in good working order;
- you have been drinking alcohol or show any signs of impairment from alcohol or drugs;
- your driving skills are not good enough to finish the test without risking the safety of yourself, the examiner or other road users, including cyclists and pedestrians.

You will not be asked to do anything illegal during the road test. The examiner will explain the test and you should simply follow her or his instructions. The examiner is not allowed to coach you during the test, so if you have any questions, ask them before you begin.

While the Level One road test checks your basic driving skills, the Level Two road test is much more demanding. You should learn the proper driving skills as soon as possible after becoming a Level One driver so you can get as much driving experience as you can before taking the Level Two test.

For the Level Two test, you must demonstrate a high level of driving skill and knowledge. You will also have to show that you can drive well on a freeway or high speed highway.

While you are taking the test, the examiner will be watching to see how well you control your vehicle and perform such driving tasks as starting, stopping, turning, parallel parking and three-point turning. The examiner will check your observation skills, including when and how often you use the mirrors, where you look, and how you respond to traffic, signs, pavement markings and possible hazards.

You will be tested on how well you manage the space around your vehicle, your ability to make safe lane changes and how closely you follow and stop behind other vehicles. How you communicate with other road users — using turn signals and brake lights and making eye contact with other drivers and pedestrians — will also be noted, as well as the correctness of your driving decisions, such as knowing when to yield the right-of-way. For more information on the Level Two road test, see Chapter 6.

At the end of each test, the examiner will give you a complete report of your skills and explain any mistakes you have made. If you fail the test, the report will show you where you need to improve. When you have had more practice, you can make an appointment to take the test again. You must wait at least 10 days between tests.

New Ontario residents

If you are a new resident of Ontario and have a valid driver's licence from another province or country, you can use that licence for 60 days in Ontario. If you want to continue to drive after 60 days, you must get an Ontario driver's licence.

Drivers from Canada, the United States and Japan

If you are a licensed driver with two or more years of driving experience in another Canadian province or territory, the United States or Japan, you may get full Class G licence privileges without taking a knowledge test or any road test. However, you must meet all medical requirements, including a vision test and show acceptable proof of your previous licence status and driving experience. These conditions also apply to licensed motorcycle drivers from Canada and the United States. However, there is no exchange agreement for motorcycle drivers from Japan.

If you have less than two years of driving experience, you may get credit for your experience and enter Level Two of the graduated licensing system. Once you have a total of two years of driving experience, you may take the Level Two road test to earn full driving privileges.

Drivers from other areas

If you are a licensed driver from a country other than Canada, the United States or Japan, you must meet the Ontario driver medical requirements, pass a vision test and a test of your knowledge of the rules of the road and traffic signs.

If you have acceptable proof of two or more years of driving experience, you may take the Level Two road test to earn full driving privileges. If you do not pass this road test, you will get a Level One (car or motorcycle) licence and may immediately schedule a Level One road test.

If you have less than two years of driving experience, you will be placed in Level One. However, if you have acceptable proof that you have the driving experience required for Level One, you can immediately schedule a Level One road test to enter Level Two.

If you do not have the driving experience required for Level One, you will stay in Level One until you do. You can then take the Level One road test to enter Level Two.

A driver's licence from another area is considered acceptable proof if it shows you have the driving experience required. If it does not, you will need to show documents that do.

If you do not have acceptable proof of your driving experience, you will start at the beginning of Level One as a new driver.

COULD YOU PASS?

The rest of this handbook gives you information you need to pass your tests and to keep your driving privileges once you get your licence.

Here is a sample question that could appear on the knowledge test:

If you are convicted of drinking and driving, you will lose your driver's licence on the first offence for a minimum of: (choose one)

1. One month.
2. Three months.
3. Six months.
4. One year.

The test may also ask you about:

- seat belts
- traffic signs and lights
- emergency vehicles
- how to use headlights
- speed limits
- getting on or off a freeway
- what drivers must do when they meet streetcars and school buses
- driver licence suspensions
- the demerit point system
- passing other vehicles
- collision reporting

The road tests will test how well you use your knowledge. You will be tested on:

- starting, stopping and turning
- traffic signs and lights
- passing vehicles, including bicycles, and driving in passing lanes
- travelling through controlled and uncontrolled intersections
- parallel parking and reversing
- foreseeing hazardous conditions and being ready for them
- other safe driving practices.

Make sure you know the information in this handbook before you take these tests.

SAFE AND RESPONSIBLE DRIVING

Being a safe and responsible driver takes a combination of knowledge, skill and attitude.

To begin, you must know the traffic laws and driving practices that help traffic move safely. Breaking these "rules of the road" is the major cause of collisions.

Traffic laws are made by federal, provincial and municipal governments, and police from each level can enforce them. If you break a traffic law, you may be fined, sent to jail or lose your driver's licence.

But you need to do more than just obey the rules. You must care about the safety of others on the road. Everyone is responsible for avoiding collisions. Even if someone else does something wrong, you may be found responsible for a collision if you could have done something to avoid it.

Because drivers have to co-operate to keep traffic moving safely, you must also be predictable, doing what other people using the road expect you to do. And you must be courteous. Courteous driving means giving other drivers space to change lanes, not cutting them off and signalling your turns and lane changes properly.

Finally, you must be able to see dangerous situations before they happen and to respond quickly and effectively to prevent them. This is called defensive or strategic driving.

Defensive driving is based on three ideas: visibility, space and communication.

Visibility is about seeing and being seen. You should always be aware of traffic in front, behind and beside you. Keep your eyes constantly moving, scanning the road ahead and to the side and checking your mirrors every five seconds or so. Make sure other drivers can see you too.

Managing the **space** around your vehicle lets you see and be seen and gives you time and space to avoid a collision. Leave a cushion of space ahead, behind and to both sides. Because the greatest risk of a collision is in front of you, stay well back.

Communicate with other road users to make sure they see you and know what you are doing. Catch the eye of pedestrians, cyclists, and drivers at intersections and signal whenever you want to slow down, stop, turn or change lanes. If you need to get another person's attention, use your horn.

I. Getting ready to drive

Before you drive, make sure you are comfortable with your physical and mental state, your vehicle and the conditions in which you will be driving. If you have doubts about any of them, don't drive.

Be physically and mentally alert

You must be in good physical and mental condition to drive.

Don't drive when you are sick or injured or when you have been drinking alcohol or taking any drug or medication that may reduce your ability to drive.

Don't drive when you are tired. You might fall asleep at the wheel, risking the lives of others on the road. Even if you don't fall asleep, fatigue affects your driving ability. Your thinking slows down and you miss seeing things. In an emergency, you may make the wrong decision or you may not make the right one fast enough.

And don't drive when you are upset or angry. Strong emotions can reduce your ability to think and react quickly.

Diagram 2-1

Know your vehicle

Get to know your vehicle before you drive it. There are many types of vehicles available today with many different characteristics. Check the vehicle owner's manual. The book Road Worthy can also help you with this.

Make sure you know where all the controls and instruments are and what they do. Check that all warning lights and gauges work. Watch for a warning light that stays on after you drive away; it could mean a serious problem with your vehicle.

Get to know the controls well enough to turn on wipers and washers, headlights, highbeams, heater and defroster without having to look. This is an important part of driving — learning to use simple controls without taking your eyes off the road.

Get into position

Make sure you sit properly behind the wheel. Your body should fit firmly against the seat back. Adjust the seat so your feet reach the pedals easily. To check your position, try placing your feet flat on the floor under the brake pedal. If you can do this without stretching, you are seated properly. If you have a headrest on your seat, raise it directly behind your head to protect you in a collision.

Check that you have enough room in the front seat to drive properly and safely. Don't overcrowd your driving space with passengers or property.

Keep a clear view

Keep a clear view when driving. Do not put anything in your windows that will block your view. If you are a new driver using the 'N' sign in your rear window, be sure it does not block your view.

The windows of your vehicle should not be coated with any material that keeps you from seeing out in any direction. Neither should the windshield or front door windows be coated to keep someone from seeing inside the vehicle.

Find your blind spots

Check and adjust your mirrors and find your blind spots. When you use mirrors there is an area on each side of your vehicle where you cannot see. You may not see people, cyclists, or vehicles when they are in these spots. Turning your head to look over your shoulder is the only way to make sure there is nothing in your blind spots. Blind spots are usually to the back left and back right of the vehicle. You should know where the blind spots are on your vehicle.

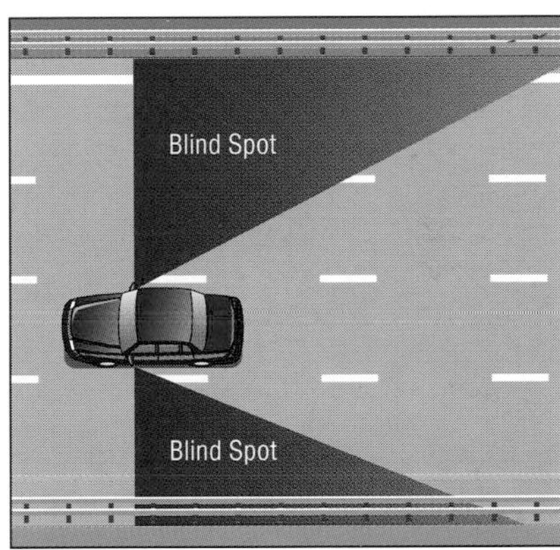

Diagram 2-2

I. Getting ready to drive

Fasten your seat belt

Never drive without first fastening your own seat belt and the seat belt or child safety seat of any passenger under 16 years old.

As a driver, you must make sure all seat belts work. Level One and Level Two drivers must make sure everyone in the vehicle has a working seat belt.

Drivers who do not buckle up can be fined up to $500 and given two demerit points. (See page 85 for information about demerit points.) You may also get demerit points if your passengers under 16 years old are not buckled into seat belts or correct child safety seats. Older passengers are responsible for their own seat belt use.

Level One and Level Two drivers who don't meet the seat belt requirements for their licence level can lose their licence for 30 days.

To work well and prevent injuries, seat belts should be snug enough to keep you firmly in your seat. Do not wear the shoulder strap under your arm where it could crush vital organs in a collision.

Diagram 2-3

The lap belt should be worn low enough on your hips to let your back move and flex. Pull the belt down low so it does not ride on your abdomen. Never put two people into one seat belt; this can cause serious injury in a collision.

Airbags do not replace seat belts. In a collision, your seat belt will keep you in position so that the airbag can protect you.

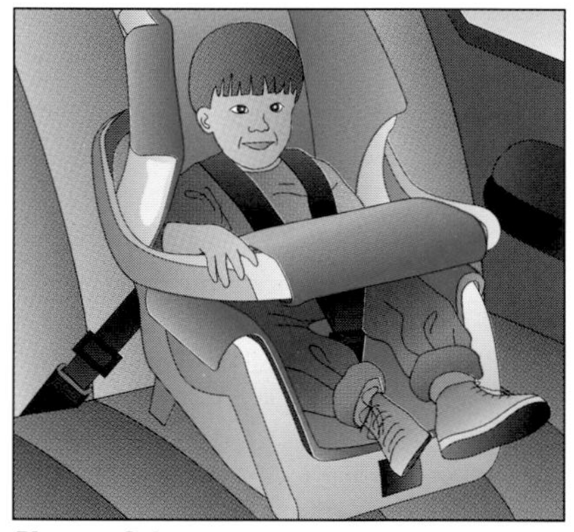

Diagram 2-4

Babies that weigh less than nine kilograms must be buckled into a rear-facing child safety seat attached to the vehicle by a seat belt. Do not put a rear-facing child safety seat in a seat protected by an airbag. If the airbag inflates, it could put pressure on the child's seat back.

Toddlers of nine to 18 kilograms travelling in their parent's vehicle must be buckled into a child safety seat attached to the vehicle both at the top by a strap and at the base by a seat belt. In any other vehicle, toddlers can use a seat belt.

Children weighing more than 18 kilograms must use seat belts. Make sure the seat belt fits snugly to the body with the lap belt below the abdomen. A booster seat may help if the shoulder belt cuts across the child's neck. A child is too big for a booster seat if it lifts the child's head and neck above the seat back, leaving the child unprotected from whiplash.

Child safety seats must meet Canadian safety standards. Buckles and straps must be placed and fastened according to the manufacturer's instructions.

For more information, read the booklets What You Should Know About Seat Belts and Choosing and Using Child Safety Seats. (Available by calling MTO Info (416) 235-4686 or 1 800 268-4648)

SEAT BELTS SAVE LIVES

Seat belts and child safety seats reduce the risk of injury or death in collisions.

- Seat belts help keep you behind the wheel and in control of the vehicle in a collision. In a vehicle with airbags, a seat belt keeps you in your seat so the airbag can protect you.
- Seat belts keep your head and body from hitting the inside of the vehicle or another person in the vehicle. When a vehicle hits a solid object the people inside keep moving until something stops them. If you are not wearing your seat belt, the steering wheel, windshield, dashboard or another person might be what stops you. This "human collision" often causes serious injury.
- Seat belts keep you inside the vehicle in a collision. People who are thrown from a vehicle have a much lower chance of surviving a collision.
- Fire or sinking in water are rare in collisions. If they do happen, seat belts help keep you conscious and unhurt, giving you a chance to get out of the vehicle.
- In a sudden stop or swerve, no one can hold onto a child who is not in a seat belt or child seat. Infants or children who are not wearing seat belts can be thrown against the vehicle's interior, collide with other people or be thrown onto the road.

I. Getting ready to drive

Turn on headlights at night and in poor conditions

Headlights make it easier for you to see and be seen at night and in poor light conditions. Your vehicle's headlights must shine a white light that can be seen at least 150 metres in front and is strong enough to light up objects 110 metres away. You must also have red rear lights that can be seen 150 metres away and a white light lighting the rear licence plate when headlights are on.

Turn on headlights one-half hour before sunset and keep them on until one-half hour after sunrise. You must also use lights when fog, snow or rain keep you from clearly seeing people or vehicles less than 150 metres away.

Don't drive with only one headlight or with lights that are not aimed properly. Have your headlight adjustment checked regularly, keep them clean, and replace burned-out bulbs as soon as possible.

Parking lights are only for parking. In low light, use your headlights, not parking lights.

When you use highbeam headlights, remember to switch to lowbeams within 150 metres of an oncoming vehicle. Use your lowbeams when you are less than 60 metres behind another vehicle unless you are passing it. These rules apply to all roads, including divided ones.

Studies show that using daytime running lights makes it easier for other drivers to see you. Remember to switch to regular headlights one-half hour before sunset.

Diagram 2-5: Highbeams

Diagram 2-6: Lowbeams

II. Driving along

Always be aware of traffic around you as you drive. Develop a routine for looking ahead, behind and from side to side. Check your mirrors every five seconds or so, and check your blind spots by turning your head to look over your shoulder. Keep other drivers out of your blind spot by changing your speed and don't drive in other vehicles' blind spots. Be extra careful at dusk and dawn when everyone has difficulty adjusting to the changing light.

Keep a cushion of space around your vehicle and be prepared for the unexpected. Anticipate other driver's movements and make allowances for every possible error. Look well ahead and watch for people in parked vehicles — they may be about to pull out in front of you or to open a door. Watch for smaller vehicles, bicycles and pedestrians.

Steer smoothly

All steering should be smooth and precise. You should do most steering and lane changes without taking either hand off the wheel. You should also be able to steer in a straight line while shifting gears, adjusting controls or checking your blind spot.

Picture the steering wheel as a clock and place your hands at nine o'clock and three o'clock or at 10 o'clock and two o'clock.

Use signals

Signals tell other drivers what you want to do, giving them a chance to co-operate.

Use your turn signals and brake lights to signal before stopping, slowing down suddenly, turning, changing lanes, leaving the road, or moving out from a parked position. Give the correct signal well before the action and make sure other

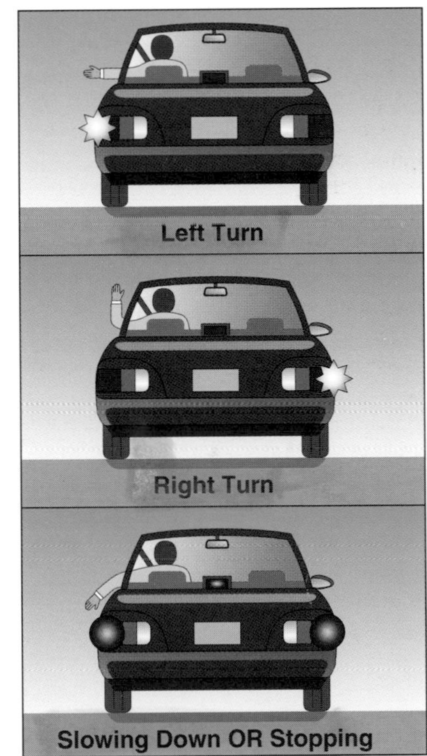

Diagram 2-7

drivers can see it. Check that the way is clear before you act — just signalling is not enough.

If your turn signals and brake lights are not working, use hand and arm signals. The pictures on page 21 show how to make hand and arm signals. When watching for signals made by others, remember that cyclists may signal right turns by holding their right arms straight out.

After signalling, move only when it is safe to do so.

Keep right

Keep to the right of the road or in the right-hand lane on multi-lane roads unless you want to turn left or pass another vehicle. This is especially important if you are driving more slowly than other vehicles.

Obey speed limits

Obey the maximum speed limit posted on signs along the road, but always drive at a speed that will let you stop safely. This means driving below the maximum speed in bad weather, in heavy traffic or in a construction zone.

Where there are no posted speed limits, the maximum speed is 50 km/h in cities, towns, villages and built-up areas and 80 km/h elsewhere.

Obey police

When police officers are directing traffic, you must follow their directions even if they are different from traffic lights or signs.

Bring your vehicle to a safe stop when a police officer signals you to pull over.

Keep a safe distance from other vehicles

As a general rule, drive at the same speed as traffic around you without going over the speed limit. Leave a cushion of space around your vehicle to let other drivers see you and to avoid a collision.

Whenever you follow another vehicle, you need enough space to stop safely if the other vehicle brakes suddenly. A safe following distance is at least two seconds behind the vehicle in front of you. This lets you see around the vehicle ahead and gives you enough distance to stop suddenly.

Do not block the normal and reasonable movement of traffic.

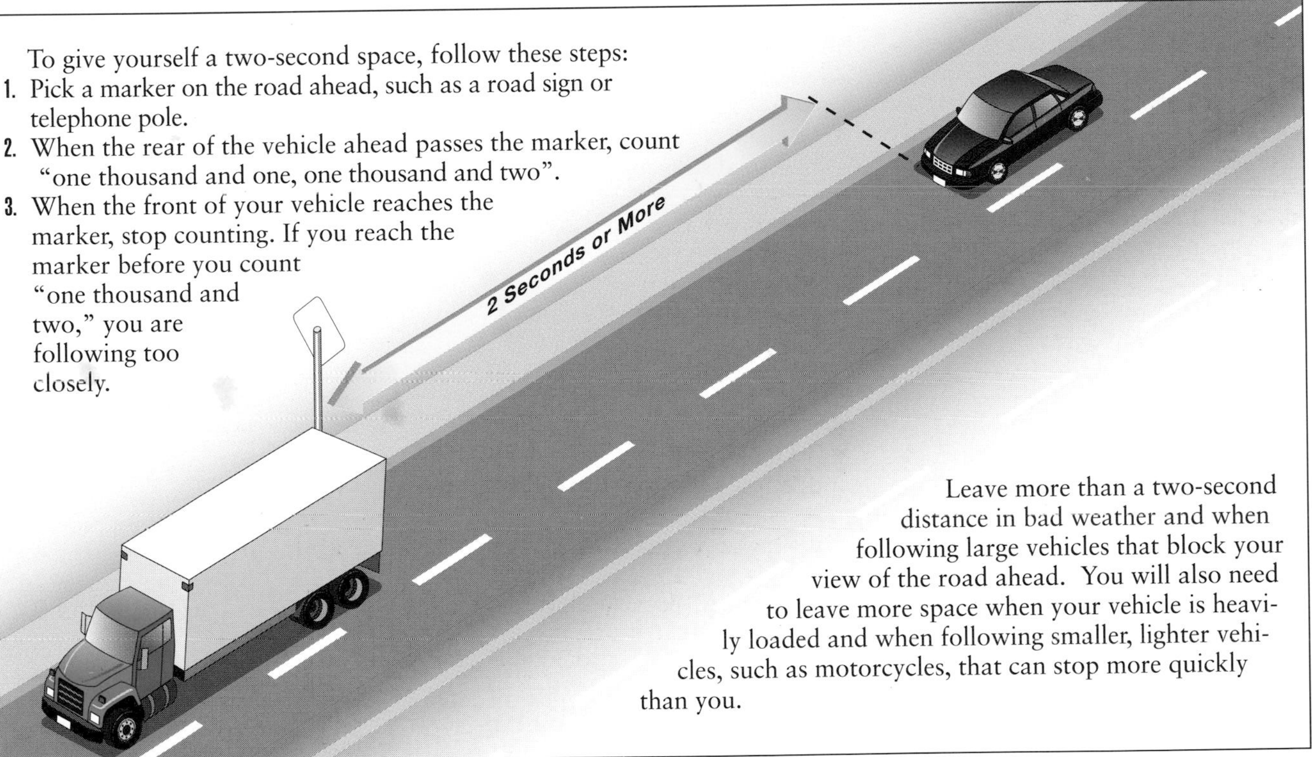
To give yourself a two-second space, follow these steps:
1. Pick a marker on the road ahead, such as a road sign or telephone pole.
2. When the rear of the vehicle ahead passes the marker, count "one thousand and one, one thousand and two".
3. When the front of your vehicle reaches the marker, stop counting. If you reach the marker before you count "one thousand and two," you are following too closely.
2 Seconds or More
Leave more than a two-second distance in bad weather and when following large vehicles that block your view of the road ahead. You will also need to leave more space when your vehicle is heavily loaded and when following smaller, lighter vehicles, such as motorcycles, that can stop more quickly than you.

Diagram 2-8

Diagram 2-9

Diagram 2-10

Share the road with smaller vehicles

Motorcycles, bicycles and mopeds are harder to see because of their size. Drivers of these vehicles may make sudden moves because of uneven road surfaces or poor weather conditions. And because they are less protected, they are more likely to be injured in a collision.

Drivers of motorcycles, bicycles and mopeds must obey the same rules of the road as car drivers. However, mopeds and bicycles that cannot keep up with traffic should drive as close as possible to the right edge of the road. For safety, cyclists should ride at least one metre away from parked vehicles and at least one-half metre away from the curb to avoid debris, potholes and sewer grates. If the lane is wide enough, you may share it with the cyclist, keeping a safe distance to the cyclist's left. If the lane is not wide enough to share, the cyclist has the right to use the whole lane.

Motorcycles use a full lane; treat them like other vehicles when driving. Since many motorcycle turn signals do not automatically shut off, be careful when turning left in front of an oncoming motorcycle with its turn signal on. Make sure the motorcyclist is turning and not going through your path having forgotten to switch off the turn signal.

Share the road with large vehicles

The length and width of large trucks can create special driving situations. For example, drivers of long trucks that are turning right may move into the left lane to avoid hitting the curb as they turn. If you ignore a truck's turn signals and pull up on its right side, you may be squeezed between the truck and the curb when the turn begins.

Most trucks need a longer distance to stop than cars. Signal well before turning, slowing or stopping to give trucks behind you enough time to brake. When stopped going uphill, a truck may roll back farther than a car when the driver releases the brake and engages the clutch. Leave at least one car length between your vehicle and the truck.

On some high-speed roads with more than two lanes in each direction, trucks longer than 6.5 metres cannot use the far left lane. Overhead signs mark these lanes. Trucks must use the lane to the right to pass slower vehicles, so try to keep this lane clear.

On some roads, buses have special stopping areas for dropping off and picking up passengers. You must let buses re-enter traffic from these areas.

Sharing the road with pedestrians

Pay special attention to pedestrians, whether they are crossing roads in traffic, walking or jogging alongside roads, or using crosswalks or pedestrian crossings. Elderly pedestrians or those with disabilities need extra caution and courtesy from drivers as they may be slow in crossing the road. Do not startle blind or visually impaired pedestrians using white canes or guide dogs by honking your horn or shouting. Caution signs are posted in some areas where there is a special need for drivers to be alert.

Some streetcar stops have a special safety island or zone for passengers getting on and off. Pass these safety islands and zones at a reasonable speed. Always be ready in case pedestrians make sudden or unexpected moves.

III. Driving through intersections

Slow down as you come to intersections and look carefully for traffic, yield signs, stop signs, traffic lights, cyclists and pedestrians.

There are two main types of intersections: controlled and uncontrolled.

Controlled intersections

Controlled intersections have traffic lights, yield signs or stop signs to control traffic.

At a controlled intersection where you face a green light, drive carefully through the intersection at a steady speed. If the light has been green for a while, be prepared to stop when it turns yellow. However, if you are already so close that you cannot stop safely, drive through the intersection with caution. Where you face a red light, come to a complete stop and wait until the light turns green.

III. Driving through intersections

When you approach an intersection on a main road, and the road beyond the side street is blocked with traffic, stop before entering the intersection and wait until the traffic ahead moves on. This does not apply if you are turning left or right.

At a controlled intersection where you face a yield sign, slow down or stop if necessary and wait until the way is clear before driving through the intersection.

At a controlled intersection where you face a stop sign, come to a complete stop. Drive through the intersection only when the way is clear.

Uncontrolled intersections

Uncontrolled intersections have no signs or traffic lights. They are usually found in areas where there is not much traffic. Be extra careful around these intersections.

If two vehicles come to an uncontrolled intersection from different roads at the same time, the driver on the left must let the driver on the right go first. This is called yielding the right-of-way.

Yield the right-of-way

There are times when you must yield the right-of-way. This means you must let another person go first. Here are some rules about when you must yield the right-of-way.

At an intersection without signs or lights, you must yield the right-of-way to any vehicle approaching from the right. (Diagram 2-11)

At an intersection with stop signs at all corners, you must yield the right-of-way to the first vehicle to come to a complete stop. If two vehicles stop at the same time, the vehicle on the left must yield to the vehicle on the right. (Diagram 2-12)

Diagram 2-11

Diagram 2-12

Diagram 2-13

At any intersection where you want to turn left or right, you must yield the right-of-way. If you are turning left, you must wait for approaching traffic to pass or turn and for pedestrians in your path to cross. If you are turning right, you must wait for pedestrians to cross if they are in your path. (Diagram 2-13)

A yield sign means you must slow down or stop if necessary and yield the right-of-way to traffic in the intersection or on the intersecting road.

Diagram 2-14

When entering a road from a private road or driveway, you must yield to vehicles on the road and pedestrians on the sidewalk. (Diagram 2-14)

Diagram 2-15

You must yield the right-of-way to pedestrians crossing at specially marked pedestrian crossings or crossovers. (Diagram 2-15)

Remember, signalling does not give you the right-of-way. You must make sure the way is clear.

IV. Stopping

Knowing how to stop safely and properly is an important driving skill. Good drivers see stops ahead, check their mirrors and begin braking early, stopping smoothly. Braking is easier when you sit properly. Use your right foot for both brake and gas pedals so you won't step on both pedals at the same time or flash your brake lights unnecessarily. Press the brake pedal firmly and evenly.

In a vehicle with manual transmission, try shifting into a lower gear going down long, steep hills. This will help control your speed and you won't have to brake as sharply. Downshift before starting downhill since it may not be possible afterwards. As a guide, you should be in the same gear going downhill as uphill.

You must come to a complete stop at all stop signs and red traffic lights. Stop at the stop line if it is marked on the pavement (Diagram 2-16). If there is no stop line, stop at the crosswalk, marked or not. If there is no crosswalk, stop at the edge of the sidewalk. If there is no sidewalk, stop at the edge of the intersection (Diagram 2-17). Wait until the way is clear before entering the intersection.

Diagram 2-16

Diagram 2-17

Stopping at railway crossings

All railway crossings on public roads in Ontario are marked with large red and white 'X' signs. Watch for these signs and be prepared to stop. You may also see signs warning of railway crossings ahead. On private roads, railway crossings may not be marked, so watch carefully.

As you come to a crossing, slow down, listen and look both ways to make sure the way is clear before crossing the tracks. If a train is coming, stop at least five metres from the nearest rail. Do not cross the track until you are sure all trains have passed.

Some railway crossings have flashing signal lights and some use gates or barriers to keep drivers from crossing the tracks when a train is coming. At a railway crossing where the signal lights are flashing, stop at least five metres from the nearest rail. Do not cross until the signals stop flashing. If the crossing has a gate or barrier, wait until it rises or opens before crossing. It is dangerous and illegal to drive around, under or through a railway gate or barrier while it is being opened or closed.

Be careful in heavy traffic not to drive onto a railway crossing if you may have to stop on the tracks. Always make sure there is enough space to drive across the tracks completely before you begin to cross.

Diagram 2-18

IV. Stopping

Stopping at school crossings

You must stop for school crossing guards guiding children across a road. These guards carry red and white stop signs. Drivers who don't stop can be fined.

Stopping for school buses

All school buses in Ontario, whatever their size, are chrome yellow and display the words 'School Bus'.

No matter what direction you are travelling in, you must stop whenever you approach a stopped school bus with its upper alternating red lights flashing, unless you are on a road with a median. In that case only vehicles coming from behind must stop. (A median is a raised, lowered or earth strip dividing a road where vehicles travel in both directions.) Coming from the opposite direction, stop at a safe distance for children to get off the bus and cross the road in front of you. If you are coming from behind the bus, stop at least 20 metres away. Do not go until the bus moves or the lights have stopped flashing.

You must obey the school bus law on any road, no matter how many lanes or what the speed limit. Be prepared to stop for a school bus at any time, not just within school hours.

As well as the upper alternating red flashing lights, school buses use a stop sign arm on the driver's side of the bus. This arm, a standard stop

Diagram 2-19

Diagram 2-20

sign with alternating flashing red lights at top and bottom, swings out after the upper alternating red lights begin to flash. Do not go until the arm folds away and all lights stop flashing.

If you don't stop for a school bus, you can be fined $400 to $2,000 and get six demerit points for a first offence. If you break the rule a second time within five years, the penalty is a fine of $1,000 to $4,000 and six demerit points. You could also go to jail for up to six months.

Watch for school buses near railway crossings. All school buses must stop at all railway crossings. The upper alternating red lights are not used for these stops, so be alert.

Stopping for pedestrian crossings

Pedestrian crossings — also called "crossovers" — let pedestrians safely cross roads where there are no traffic lights. Always watch for pedestrians and people using wheelchairs near these crossings. At some crossings, pedestrians can push a button to make overhead yellow lights flash; at all crossings, pedestrians should point across the road to show they want to cross. Drivers, including cyclists, must stop and let all pedestrians cross. Once people have cleared your side of the road you can go with caution.

Diagram 2-21

Never pass another vehicle that has stopped to let people cross the road.

V. Changing directions

Before you turn a corner, back up or turn around, always check your mirrors and over your shoulder to make sure the way is clear and you have enough space to complete the move safely.

Turning a corner

To turn a corner, signal well before the turn. When the way is clear, move into the proper lane — either the far right lane for a right turn or the far left lane in your direction for a left turn. Signal your turn and look from side to side to make sure the way is clear.

Slow down before you enter the turn; the sharper the turn, the slower you should go. To keep full control of the turn, finish braking before you turn the steering wheel.

For a sharp turn, turn the steering wheel with one hand and cross the other hand over it. Grip the wheel on the other side and continue turning. This is called "hand over hand steering." When you have completed the turn, relax your grip on the steering wheel and let it slip or gently feed it through your hands to return to the straight-ahead position. Do not turn the steering wheel with one finger or the flat palm of your hand.

Gradually increase speed as you complete the turn.

Remember, drivers lose control of vehicles and skid because they try to do more than one thing at a time. Try not to brake and steer at the same time.

Diagram 2-22

Right turns

Unless signs or pavement markings tell you not to, always begin and end a right turn close to the right side of the road.

To make a right turn, signal well before the turn and move into the right-hand lane when the way is clear. If the right-hand lane is not marked, keep as far to the right of the road as possible. Look ahead, left, right and left again before starting to turn. If you may not have seen any smaller vehicles or pedestrians, check your right rear blind spot. Let cyclists or moped riders go through the intersection before you turn. When it is safe, make your turn into the right-hand lane of the road.

Right turn on a red light

You may turn right on a red light as long as you first come to a complete stop and wait until the way is clear. Remember to yield to pedestrians and others using the road.

Left turns

Unless signs or pavement markings tell you not to, always begin and end a left turn in the far left lane in your direction.

To make a left turn, signal well before the turn and move into the far left lane when the way is clear. Look ahead, left, right and left again and check your blind spot. Make your turn when the way is clear.

When you are stopped at an intersection waiting for approaching traffic to clear, don't turn your steering wheel to the left until you can complete the turn. With your wheels turned to the left, your vehicle could be pushed into the path of oncoming traffic.

When two vehicles coming from opposite directions meet in an intersection waiting to turn left, each should turn to the left of the other after yielding the right-of-way to pedestrians and oncoming traffic.

Motorcycles, bicycles and mopeds turn left at intersections in the same way as larger vehicles. If you are making a left turn behind one of these vehicles, do not pull up beside it to make your turn at the same time. Stay behind and turn when the way is clear. Wait for the smaller vehicle to move right before you pass.

The following diagrams show you the correct way to turn left on different types of roads:

V. Changing directions

Diagram 2-23: Two-way road to a two-way road.

Turn from the lane closest to the centre line to the lane right of the centre line, following a smooth arc. Then, when you can, move into the right curb lane.

Diagram 2-24: Two-way road to a one-way road.

Turn from the lane closest to the centre line to the left curb lane.

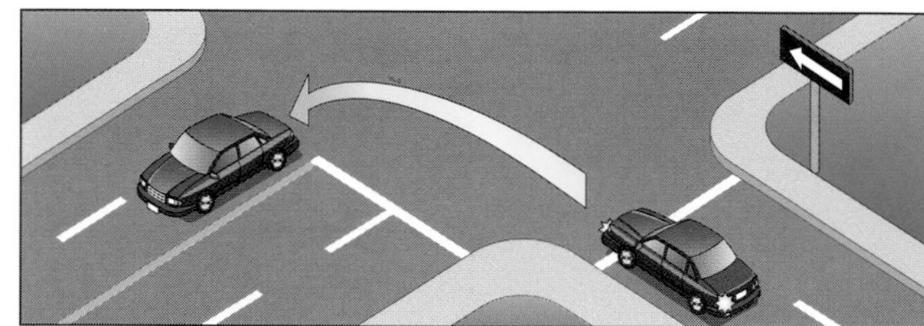

Diagram 2-25: One-way road to a two-way road.

Turn from the left curb lane to the lane just right of the centre line. Then, when you can, move into the right curb lane.

Diagram 2-26: One-way road to a one-way road.

Turn from the left curb lane to the left curb lane.

Left-turn lanes

Some roads have special lanes for vehicles turning left. **(Diagram 2-27)** At an intersection where left-turn lanes are marked on the pavement, make your turn from the marked lane. Keep this lane position as you turn onto the other road.

The centre lane of some roads is used as a two-way left-turn lane. **(Diagram 2-28)** This lets left-turning vehicles from both directions wait for a chance to turn without holding up traffic. To use a two-way left-turn lane, follow these steps:

1. Signal and move into the centre lane shortly before your turn. Slow down.
2. Carefully move forward to a spot opposite the road or driveway where you want to turn.
3. Make your turn when the way is clear.

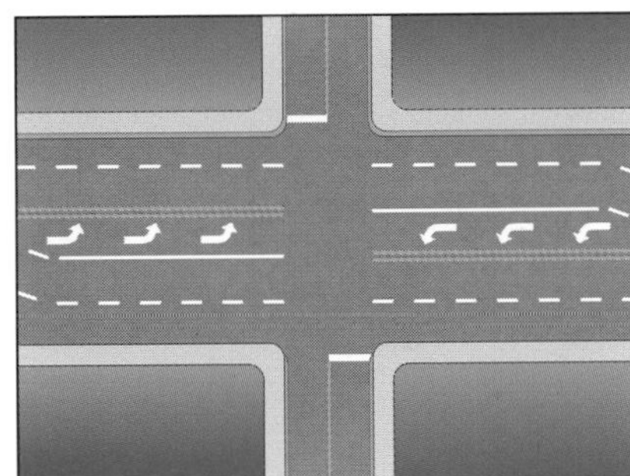

Diagram 2-27

Remember that vehicles from the opposite direction also use this lane to turn left. As they wait in front of you, it may be hard for you to see oncoming traffic. Only go when you are sure the way is clear.

Left turn on a red light

You may turn left from a one-way road to a one-way road on a red light after coming to a complete stop and making sure the way is clear. Yield to pedestrians and traffic.

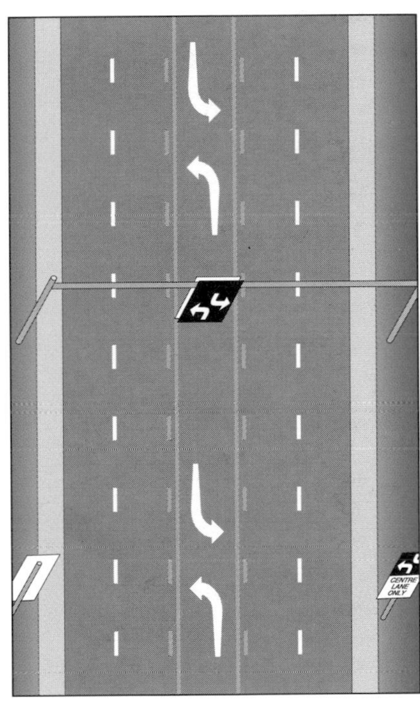

Diagram 2-28

V. Changing directions

Backing up

Take extra care and move slowly when backing up (reversing) your vehicle. Before you begin, check that the way is clear behind you. Be especially careful to look for children and cyclists. Put the gear selector in reverse and turn sideways in your seat to look over your shoulder in the direction you are moving, while holding the steering wheel firmly.

If you are reversing straight back or to the right, turn your body and head to the right and look back over your right shoulder. **(Diagram 2-29)** When reversing to the left, turn your body and head to the left and look over your left shoulder. **(Diagram 2-30)** Always check the opposite shoulder as well. If you are turning as you reverse, check that the front end of your vehicle does not hit anything.

You don't have to wear a seat belt while backing up. If you need to remove your seat belt to turn your body to see properly when reversing, do so. But don't forget to buckle up again before moving forward.

Diagram 2-29

It is illegal to drive in reverse on a divided road that has a speed limit of more than 80 km/h. This applies to the travelled section of the road and the shoulder. The only exception to this rule is if you are trying to help someone in trouble.

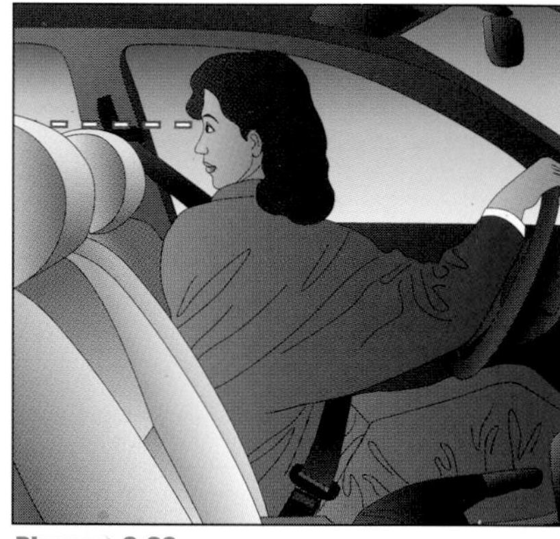

Diagram 2-30

Turning around

You may need to turn around when driving if you miss a turn or go too far along a road. There are several ways to do this safely.

The simplest and safest way is to drive around the block, but there may be times when this is not possible. In such cases, a U-turn or a three-point turn may be necessary.

U-turn

Before you make a U-turn, check to make sure there is no sign saying not to.

To make a U-turn safely, you must be able to see well in both directions. It is illegal to make a U-turn on a curve in the road, on or near a railway crossing or hilltop, or near a bridge or tunnel that blocks your view. Never make a U-turn unless you can see at least 150 metres in both directions.

To make a U-turn, signal for a right turn, check your mirror and over your shoulder and pull over to the right side of the road. Stop. Signal a left turn and when traffic is clear in both directions, move forward and turn quickly and sharply into the opposite lane. Check for traffic as you turn.

Three-point turn

On narrow roads you need to make a three-point turn to change directions. As shown in **Diagram 2-31**, a three-point turn starts from the far right side of the road.

Signal for a left turn. When the way is clear in both directions, move forward, turning the steering wheel sharply left towards the curb on the far side of the road. When you have reached the left side of the road, stop, and put the vehicle into reverse. Signal a right turn. After checking that the way is still clear, turn the steering wheel sharply to the right, while backing up slowly to the other side of the road. Stop. Shift to forward gear and check traffic. When the way is clear, drive forward.

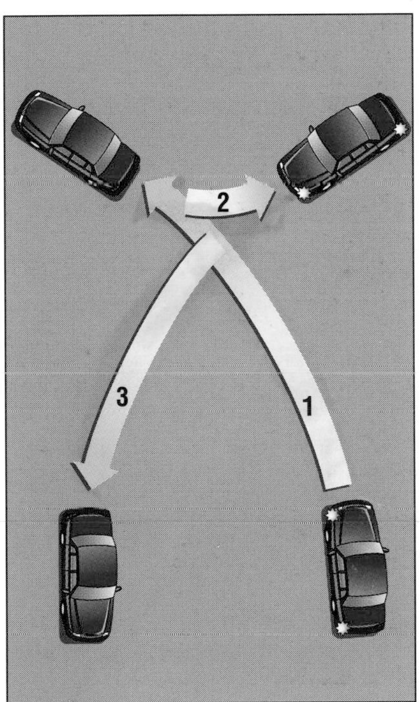

Diagram 2-31

VI. Changing positions

Changing your position on the road involves changing lanes or overtaking and passing another vehicle. Before beginning, be sure you have enough space and time to complete the move safely.

Changing lanes

Changing lanes is a sideways movement from one lane to another on roads with two or more lanes in the same direction. You may want to change lanes to overtake another vehicle, to avoid a parked vehicle or when the vehicle ahead slows to turn at an intersection.

Never change lanes without giving the proper signal and looking to make sure the move can be made safely.

Here are the steps for making a lane change.

1. Check your mirrors for a space in traffic where you can enter safely.
2. Check your blind spot by looking over your shoulder in the direction of the lane change. Signal that you want to move left or right.
3. Check again to make sure the way is clear and that no one is coming too fast from behind or from two lanes over on a multi-lane road.
4. Steer gradually into the new lane. Do not slow down — maintain the same speed or gently increase it.

Never make sudden lane changes by cutting in front of another vehicle, including bicycles. Other drivers expect you to stay in the lane you are already in. Even if you signal, they expect you to yield the right-of-way.

Avoid unnecessary lane changes or weaving from lane to lane. You are more likely to cause a collision, especially in heavy traffic or bad weather.

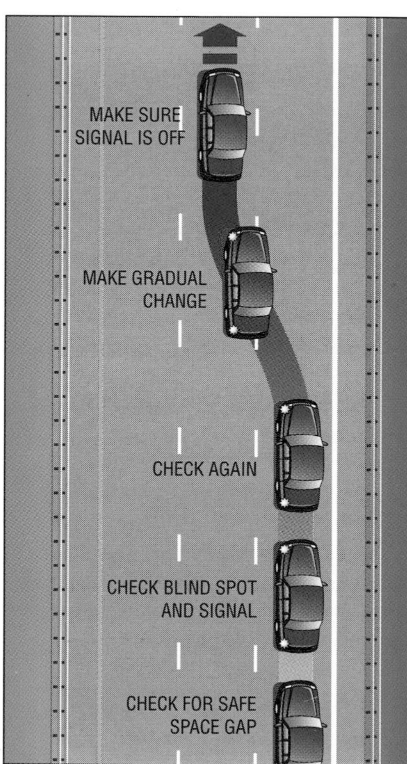

Diagram 2-32

Don't change lanes in or near an intersection. Remember that spending a few seconds behind another vehicle is often safer than going around it.

Passing

Passing is changing lanes to move past a slower vehicle. Although all roads have speed limits, not all vehicles travel at the same speed. For example, cyclists, vehicles working on the road and drivers preparing to turn are usually slower than the main traffic. You will likely want to pass some slow-moving vehicles when you are behind them.

Never overtake and pass another vehicle unless you are sure you can do so without danger to yourself or others. Don't pass moving snow plows under any conditions. If in doubt, do not pass.

Here are the steps for passing a vehicle:

1. Use your left-turn signal to show that you want to pass and check that the way is clear ahead and behind before moving into the passing lane.
2. Watch out for bicycles and small vehicles that may be hidden from view in front of the vehicle you are about to pass. Also watch for vehicles that may be turning left in front of you and vehicles or pedestrians entering the road from another road or driveway.
3. Change lanes only after signalling. After overtaking, signal that you want to move back into the lane you started from, and when you can see all of the front of the vehicle you are passing in your rear view mirror, make the lane change. Be careful not to cut off a vehicle by suddenly moving in front of it.

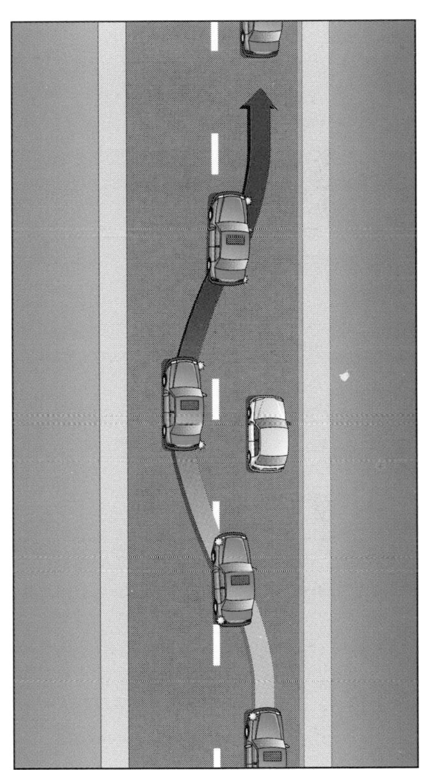

Diagram 2-33

VI. Changing positions

4. If the vehicle you are passing speeds up, do not race. Go back to your original lane. And do not speed up when another driver is trying to pass you. It is rude and dangerous.

Do not pass within 30 metres of a pedestrian crossing.

When passing parked vehicles, watch carefully for people suddenly opening doors or for doors opened to load and unload.

Motorcycles, bicycles and mopeds often need to pull to the left or right side of their lane to avoid dangerous road conditions or to be seen by other drivers. Do not take this as an invitation to pass in the same lane. If you do want to pass these vehicles, do so by changing lanes.

When another vehicle wants to pass you, you must move to the right and let it pass. When being passed on an undivided road where the passing driver has pulled into the opposite lane, pay attention to oncoming traffic and move closer to the right side of the lane. Be prepared to slow down to let the passing driver get in front of you more quickly to prevent a collision.

On many high-speed roads with three or more lanes in each direction, trucks are not allowed to drive in the far left-hand lane. This means that the lane next to it is the truck passing lane. If you are in this lane and a truck wants to pass, move into the right-hand lane as soon as you can.

Passing at night

Be very careful when you pass other vehicles at night. If you have to pass and the way is clear, follow these steps:

1. Switch your headlights to low beams as you approach a vehicle from behind.
2. Switch your highbeams on and off quickly to warn the driver

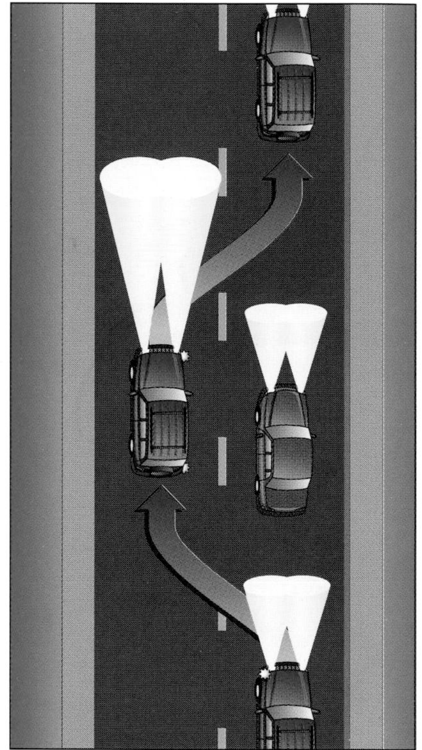

Diagram 2-34

ahead you are going to pass.

3. Signal, check your mirrors and blind spot, and pull out to pass. As you move alongside the vehicle you are passing, switch on your highbeams. This will let you see more of the road ahead.
4. When you can see all of the front of the vehicle you are passing in your rear view mirror, you are far enough ahead to pull back into the right lane. Remember to signal.

Diagram 2-35

Passing and climbing lanes

Some high-speed roads have special passing or climbing lanes. These lanes let slower vehicles move into the right-hand lane so that faster ones can pass safely in the left lane.

An advance sign tells drivers they will soon have a chance to pass. Another sign warns when the lane is ending so drivers in the right-hand lane can begin to merge safely with traffic in the left-hand lane.

VI. Changing positions

Passing on the shoulder

You may drive on the right shoulder only to pass a vehicle turning left and only if the shoulder is paved. The only exception to this is when the operator of a vehicle that is working on the road signals you to pass on the right and you can do so safely. You may not pass on the left shoulder, paved or not.

Passing on the right

Most passing is done on the left. You may pass on the right on multi-lane or one-way roads and when overtaking a streetcar or a left-turning vehicle.

Passing on the right can be more dangerous than passing on the left. If you are driving in the passing lane with a slower vehicle in front of you, wait for the vehicle to move to the right. Do not suddenly change lanes and pass on the right; the driver in front may realize you want to pass and move to the right at the same time you do.

Passing streetcars

You must pass streetcars on the right unless you are driving on a one-way road.

At streetcar stops, stay at least two metres behind the rear doors where passengers are getting off or on.

This rule does not apply at stops where an area has been set aside for streetcar passengers. Always pass these areas at a reasonable speed and be prepared for pedestrians to make sudden or unexpected moves.

Diagram 2-36

VII. Parking

Since parking rules change from road to road and place to place, always watch for and obey signs that say you may not stop or limit stopping, standing or parking. Be aware that not all parking by-laws are posted on signs.

Here are some basic parking rules:

- Never park on the travelled part of a road. Drive off the road onto the shoulder if you must stop for some reason.
- Never park on a curve, hill or anywhere you do not have a clear view for at least 125 metres in both directions.
- Do not park where you will block a vehicle already parked or where you will block a sidewalk, crosswalk, pedestrian crossing or road entrance.
- Do not park within three metres of a fire hydrant, on or within 100 metres of a bridge or within six metres of a public entrance to a hotel, theatre or public hall when it is open to the public.
- Do not park within nine metres of an intersection or within 15 metres if it is controlled by traffic lights.
- Do not park within 15 metres of the nearest rail of a level railway crossing.
- Do not park where you will get in the way of traffic or snow clearing.

Diagram 2-37

- Never open the door of your parked vehicle without first making sure that you will not endanger any other person or vehicle or interfere with traffic. When you must open a door next to traffic, keep it open only long enough to load or unload passengers.
- Never park in a space designated for people with disabilities unless you display a Disabled Person

VII. Parking

Parking Permit in the windshield of your vehicle. The permit must belong to you or one of your passengers. This also applies to standing or stopping at curb areas reserved for picking up and dropping off passengers with disabilities.

After parking your vehicle, always turn off the ignition and the lights, remove the key and lock the door to stop theft. Do not leave children or animals in the vehicle.

Before moving from a parked position, always signal and check for traffic, pulling out only when it is safe to do so.

Diagram 2-38

PARKING FOR PEOPLE WITH DISABILITIES

The Disabled Person Parking Permit, issued by the Ministry of Transportation, replaced disabled symbol licence plates and municipal parking permits in 1990.

The portable permit may be used in any vehicle in which a driver or passenger with a disability is travelling. A vehicle displaying the permit and carrying a person with a disability (either as driver or passenger) may park in designated spaces. Ontario, all other Canadian provinces, and most American states recognize the permit.

The permit is available, free of charge, to eligible applicants. To be eligible, you must be unable to walk more than 200 metres without serious difficulty or danger to safety or health. You must show a medical certificate from a licensed physician, chiropractor, osteopathic physician, physiotherapist or occupational therapist. Temporary permits are also available for people with a disability lasting more than two months but not permanent. Companies and organizations that provide transportation regularly to people with disabilities can also apply for permits. Application forms are available from your local Ministry of Transportation Driver and Vehicle Licence Issuing Office.

It is illegal to park in a parking space for people with disabilities unless you have an official parking permit and are transporting the permit holder. You must display the permit on the sun visor or dashboard in the windshield of the vehicle.

You could be fined $50 to $2,000 under municipal by-laws for unlawfully parking in a designated space. These parking spaces are marked with a Disabled Person Parking Permit sign.

Parallel parking

Parallel parking means parking vehicles in a line, front to rear, next to the curb or side of the road. Park parallel to the curb on roads where parking is allowed unless there are signs saying that vehicles should be parked at an angle. Park on the right side of the road in the direction of traffic. Unless there are signs saying otherwise, you can parallel park on both sides of a one-way road.

To parallel park on the right-hand side of the road, find a space that is about one and half times longer than your vehicle. Check the traffic beside and behind and signal your wish to pull over and stop. Drive alongside — or parallel to — the vehicle ahead of the empty space, leaving about a metre between the vehicles. Stop when your rear bumper is in line with the other vehicle.**1** Slowly and carefully reverse into the space, turning the steering wheel fully towards the curb.**2** When you can see the outside rear corner of the vehicle in front of your space, straighten your wheels as you continue to reverse.**3** Then turn the steering wheel fully toward the road to bring your vehicle in line with the curb.**4** If your vehicle is not parallel to the curb, drive forward to straighten.**5**

When you are properly parked, set the parking brake and move the gear selector into park or shift into first or reverse gear and turn off the engine. Remember to remove the key from the ignition. Check traffic before opening your door. Lock your vehicle.

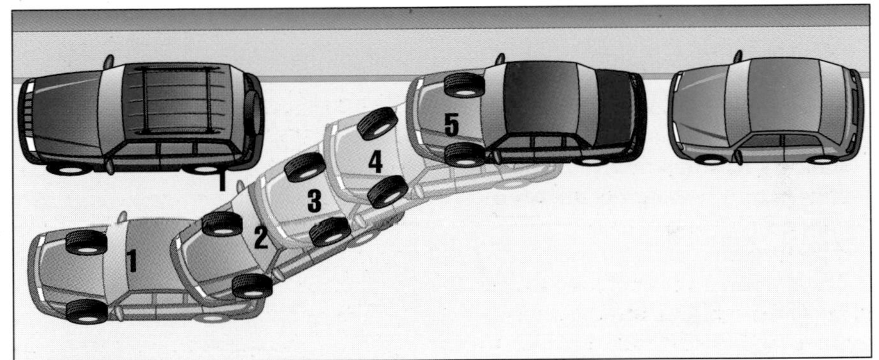

Diagram 2-39

VII. Parking

Parking on a hill

When parking facing downhill, turn your front wheels towards the curb or right shoulder. This will keep the vehicle from rolling into traffic if the brakes become disengaged. **(Diagram 2-40 A)**

Turn the steering wheel to the left so the wheels are turned towards the road if you are facing uphill with a curb. The tires will catch the curb if it rolls backward. **(Diagram 2-40 B)** Facing uphill without a curb, turn the wheels sharply to the right. If the vehicle rolls, it will go off the road rather than into traffic. **(Diagram 2-40 C)**

When parking on a hill, always set the parking brake and put the gear selector into park or shift into first or reverse gear. Turn off the engine and remove the key. Check for traffic before opening the door and remember to lock your vehicle.

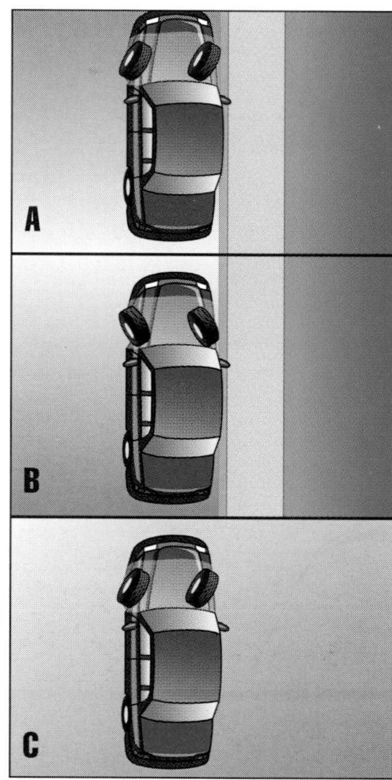

Diagram 2-40

Roadside stop

When you need to stop by the side of the road for a short time — to check something outside your vehicle or to look for directions on a map, for example — follow these directions.

Signal that you want to pull over and check your mirrors and blind spot to see when the way is clear. Steer to the side of the road, stopping close to the curb or edge of the road.

Set the parking brake. Put the gear selector into park, or shift into neutral if your vehicle has a manual transmission. Turn on your four-way emergency flashers. Turn off the engine. Take your feet off the pedals.

When pulling out from a roadside stop, turn off your flashers, release the parking brake and move the gear selector to drive or shift into first gear. Signal and check your mirrors and blind spot to make sure the way is clear of vehicles and cyclists before driving back onto the road.

VIII. Freeway driving

A freeway — also called an expressway — is a high-speed, multi-lane road. On a freeway, traffic going in each direction is separated and special ramps let vehicles enter and exit. Vehicles travel faster on a freeway than on other roads, so driving can be more demanding and difficult. However, because there are no intersections, bicycles or pedestrians, freeway driving can be safer for experienced drivers.

New drivers need to learn how to drive with other vehicles around them at low speeds before trying freeway driving. Class G1 drivers may only drive on freeways with a licensed driving instructor.

Entering a freeway

There are usually two parts to a freeway entrance: an entrance ramp and an acceleration lane. In this lane, drivers raise their speed to the common speed of traffic on the freeway before they merge with it.

As you move along the freeway entrance ramp, look ahead at the traffic and try to see where you will move into the nearest freeway lane. As you leave the ramp and enter the acceleration lane, signal and increase your speed to merge smoothly with traffic. Freeway drivers should move over, if it is safe to do so, leaving room for merging vehicles.

A few entrance ramps join the freeway on the left. This means you enter the fastest lane of traffic first. Use the acceleration lane to match your speed to the traffic, increasing your speed more quickly.

Diagram 2-41

VIII. Freeway driving

Driving along a freeway

Once on the freeway, a good safety-conscious driver moves at a steady speed, looking forward and anticipating what's going to happen on the road ahead. Traffic should keep to the right, using the left lanes for passing.

As in city driving, your eyes should be constantly moving, scanning the road ahead, to each side and behind. Look ahead to where you are going to be in the next 15 to 20 seconds, or as far ahead as you can see, when you travel at faster speeds. Remember to keep scanning and check your mirrors frequently.

Stay clear of large vehicles. Because of their size, they block your view more than other vehicles. Leave space around your vehicle. This will let you see clearly in every direction and will give you time and space to react. (See page 22 for correct following distances.)

Diagram 2-42

Be careful not to cut off any vehicle, large or small, when making a lane change or joining the flow of traffic. It is dangerous and illegal for a slower moving vehicle to cut in front of a faster moving vehicle.

Use the far left lane of a multi-lane freeway to pass traffic moving slower than the speed limit, but don't stay there. Drive in the right-hand lane when possible. On many freeways with three or more lanes in each direction, trucks cannot travel in the far left lane and must use the lane to the right for passing. Get into the habit of driving in the right lane, leaving the other lanes clear for passing.

Leaving a freeway

There are usually three parts to a freeway exit: a lane for slowing down that leads drivers out of the main flow of traffic, an exit ramp and an intersection with a stop sign, a yield sign or traffic light.

When leaving the freeway, signal that you want to move into the slowing lane, but do not slow down. When you are in the lane, reduce your speed gradually to the speed shown for the exit ramp. Check your speedometer to make sure you are going slowly enough. You may not realize how fast you are going because you are used to the high speed of the freeway. Be prepared to stop at the end of the exit ramp.

Signs tell you that there are freeway exits ahead far enough in advance for you to make any lane changes safely. If you miss an exit, do not stop or reverse on the freeway. Take the next exit.

HIGHWAY HYPNOSIS

Driving for a long time can be boring, especially at night or when you drive at the same speed for long distances. You can become "hypnotized" where everything seems to float by and you pay less attention to what is happening around you. You may even fall asleep.

You can help prevent highway hypnosis by following a few simple rules:

1. Don't eat a heavy meal before you drive.
2. Wear comfortable clothing.
3. Talk with your passengers, but not to the point of distraction.
4. Keep your eyes moving and check your mirrors often.
5. Take an interest in all road signs and traffic around you.
6. Take a coffee or walking break every hour.
7. Don't try to drive too far in one day.
8. Avoid driving during your normal sleeping hours.
9. Keep the temperature in your vehicle cool.

If you do start to become drowsy, do something different immediately. Open a window; talk to passengers; sing out loud; move your body around a bit.

Stop at the next service centre or rest area and take a short walk or have a coffee and eat a light snack. If you don't feel any more alert, find a place to sleep for an hour or for the night.

IX. Dealing with particular situations

Workers on the road

Take extra care when driving through areas where people are working on or near the road. Slow down and be prepared to stop. Obey all construction signs and any workers who are directing traffic through the area.

Treat people working on roads with respect and be patient if traffic is delayed. Sometimes traffic in one direction must wait while vehicles from the other lane pass through a detour. If your lane is blocked and no one is directing traffic, yield to the driver coming from the opposite direction. When the way is clear, move slowly and carefully around the obstacle.

Animals on the road

You may come upon farm animals or wild animals on the road, especially in farming areas and in the northern parts of the province.

Animal crossing signs warn drivers where there is a known danger of large animals, such as moose, deer or cattle, stepping onto the road, but small animals may appear anywhere. Always be alert for animals and ready to react.

Look well ahead. At night, use your highbeams where possible. When you see an animal, brake or slow down if you can without risk to vehicles behind you. If there is no traffic and no danger of colliding with any other object, steer around the animal, staying in control of your vehicle.

In some areas of the province horse-drawn carriages may use the road. Be prepared to share the road with them.

Cellular phones

Cellular phones can be an important safety aid for drivers. Many people use their phones to report crimes and collisions and for personal safety when they are lost or their vehicle breaks down.

But using a cellular phone while driving takes a driver's attention from the business of driving. Distracted drivers are more likely to make a driving error or to react too slowly. As more and more people use cellular phones, it is important that they be used safely.

Make it a habit to use your cellular phone only when you are parked, or have a passenger use the phone. If you are driving and your phone rings, let your cellular voice mail service take the call and listen to the message later when you are parked.

If you must use a cellular phone when driving, use a hands-free microphone. Make sure your phone is easy to see and reach and that you know how to use it. Use voice-activated or speed dialing and never take notes while driving.

Currently, there is no law against using a cellular phone while driving, but you can be charged with dangerous or careless driving if you cause a collision while using one.

Emergency vehicles

If you hear the bell or siren of a police, fire, ambulance or public utility emergency vehicle, or see its lights flashing, you must get out of the way. On a two-way road, stop as close as possible to the right-hand side of the road and clear of any intersection. On a one-way road with more than two lanes, stop as close as possible to the nearest edge of the road and clear of any intersection. Wait until the emergency vehicle has passed.

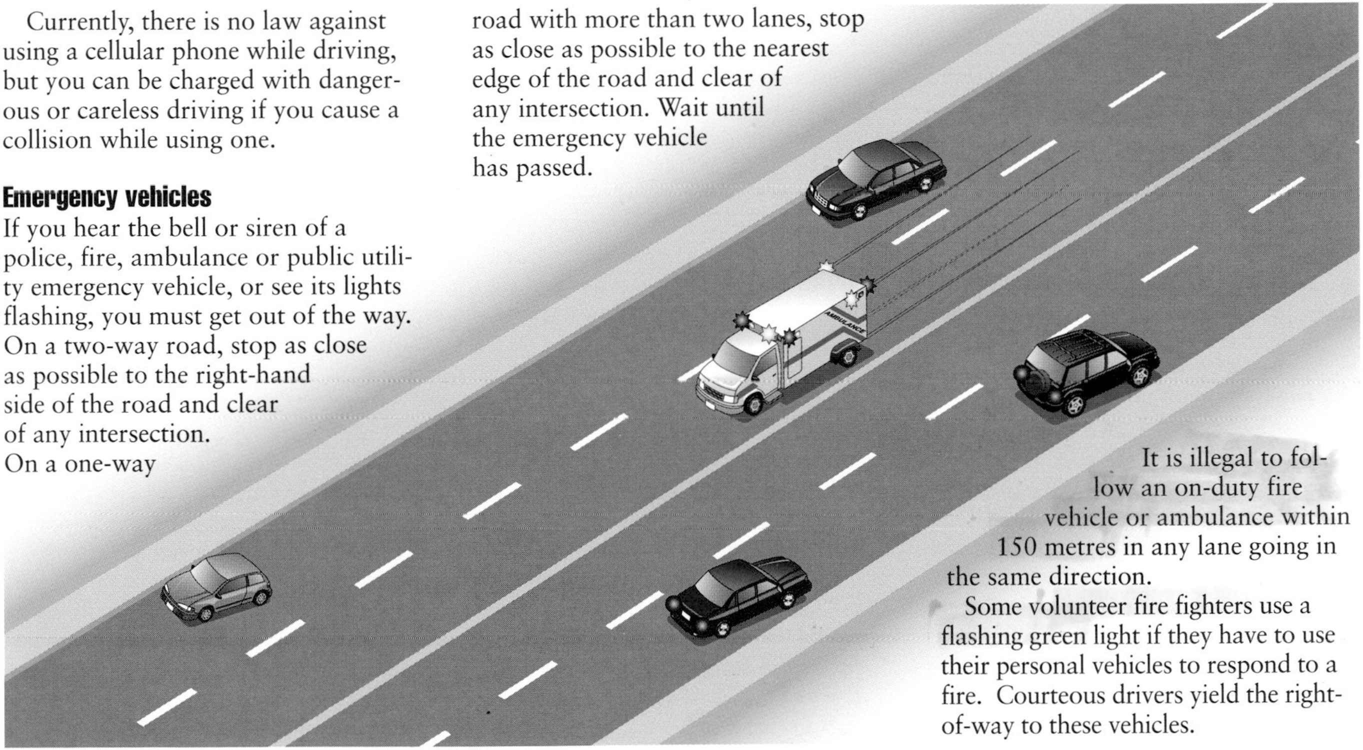

It is illegal to follow an on-duty fire vehicle or ambulance within 150 metres in any lane going in the same direction.

Some volunteer fire fighters use a flashing green light if they have to use their personal vehicles to respond to a fire. Courteous drivers yield the right-of-way to these vehicles.

Diagram 2-43

X. Driving at night and in bad weather

At night and in weather conditions such as rain, snow or fog, you cannot see as far ahead, even with headlights. Slow down when driving at night, especially on unlit roads, and whenever weather conditions reduce your visibility.

Overdriving your headlights

You are overdriving your headlights when you go so fast that your stopping distance is farther than you can see with your headlights. This is a dangerous thing to do, because you may not give yourself enough room to make a safe stop. Reflective road signs can mislead you as well, making you believe you can see farther than you really can. This may cause you to overdrive your headlights if you are not careful.

Glare

Glare is dazzling light that makes it hard for you to see and be aware what others around you are doing. It can be a problem on sunny and overcast days, depending on the angle of the sun's rays and your surroundings. Glare can also be a problem at night when you face bright headlights or see them reflected in your rear view mirror.

When meeting oncoming vehicles with bright headlights at night, look up and beyond and slightly to the right of the oncoming lights. In daytime glare, use your sun visor or keep a pair of good quality sunglasses in your vehicle. When you enter a tunnel on a bright day, slow down to let your eyes adjust to the reduced light. Remove your sunglasses and turn on your headlights.

Cut down glare at night by following the rules of the road for vehicle lights. Use your lowbeam headlights within 150 metres of an oncoming vehicle or when following a vehicle within 60 metres. On country roads,

Diagram 2-44

switch to lowbeams when you come to a curve or hilltop so you can see oncoming headlights and won't blind oncoming drivers. If you can't see any headlights, switch back to highbeams.

Fog

Fog is dangerous because it greatly reduces your vision. In fog, turn on your lights and slow down. Use your headlights on lowbeam only; highbeams reflect off the moisture droplets in the fog, making it even harder to see. Do not pass. Be patient. You can often see better when following another vehicle, but don't follow too closely.

Rain

Rain makes road surfaces slippery, especially as the first drops fall. With more rain, tires make less contact with the road. If there is too much water or if you are going too fast, your tires may ride on top of the water, like water skis. This is called hydroplaning. When this happens, control becomes very difficult. Make sure you have good tires with deep tread, and slow down when the road is wet.

Rain also reduces visibility. Drive slow enough to be able to stop within the distance you can see. Make sure your windshield wipers are in good condition. If your wiper blades do not clean the windshield without streaking, replace them.

In rain, try to drive on clear sections of road. Look ahead and plan your movements. Smooth steering, braking and accelerating will reduce the chance of skids. Leave more space between you and the vehicle ahead in case you have to stop. This will also help you to avoid spray from the vehicle ahead that can make it even harder to see.

Stay out of puddles. A puddle can hide a large pothole that could damage your vehicle or its suspension, or flatten a tire. The spray of water could splash nearby pedestrians or drown your engine, causing it to stall. Water can also make your brakes less effective.

Flooded roads

Try not to drive on flooded roads — water may prevent your brakes from working. If you must drive through a flooded stretch of road, test your brakes afterwards to dry them out.

Test your brakes when it is safe by stopping quickly and firmly at 50 km/h. Make sure the vehicle stops in a straight line, without pulling to one side. The brake pedal should feel firm and secure, not spongy — that's a sign of trouble. If you still feel a pulling to one side or a spongy brake pedal even after the brakes are dry, you should take the vehicle in for repair immediately.

Skids

A skid happens when your wheels slide out of control on a slippery surface. Skids can involve the front, rear or all four wheels. Most skids result from driving too fast for road or traffic conditions. Skids can also be caused by sudden, hard braking, going too fast around a corner or accelerating too quickly.

Once in a skid, steer in the direction of the skid. To do this, look where you want your vehicle to go and steer toward that spot. Be careful not to oversteer. If you are on ice, skidding in a straight line, step on the clutch or shift to neutral.

X. Driving at night and in bad weather

Brake to the point of locking the brakes, release and repeat. It is a good idea to practise doing this under controlled conditions with a qualified driving instructor.

If your vehicle has an anti-lock braking system, learn how to use it in an emergency. Some drivers, unfamiliar with anti-lock braking, are surprised by the vibration that happens when they brake hard in an emergency. Make sure you know what to expect so you can react quickly and effectively in an emergency.

Snow

Snow may be hard-packed and slippery as ice. It can also be rutted, full of hard tracks and gullies. Or it can be smooth and soft. Look ahead and anticipate what you must do based on the conditions. Slow down on rutted, snowy roads. Avoid sudden steering, braking or accelerating that could cause a skid.

Whiteouts

Blowing snow may create whiteouts where snow completely blocks your view of the road. When blowing snow is forecast, drive only if necessary and with extreme caution.

Ice

As temperatures drop below freezing, wet roads become icy. Sections of road, in shaded areas or on bridges and overpasses, freeze first. It is important to look ahead, slow down and anticipate.

If the road ahead looks like black and shiny asphalt, be suspicious. It may be covered by a thin layer of ice known as black ice. Generally, asphalt in the winter should look gray-white in colour. If you think there may be black ice ahead, slow down and be careful.

Snow plows

Snow removal vehicles are equipped with flashing blue lights that can be seen from 150 metres. A flashing blue light can only be used on snow removal vehicles.

Flashing blue lights warn you of wide and slow-moving vehicles: some snow plows have a wing that extends as far as three metres to the right of the vehicle. On freeways, several snow plows may be staggered across the road, clearing all lanes at the same time by passing a ridge of snow from plow to plow. Do not try to pass between them. This is extremely dangerous because there is not enough room to pass safely, and the ridge of wet snow can throw your vehicle out of control.

XI. Dealing with emergencies

If you drive often or travel alone, you need to be ready to deal with emergencies. The Ontario Provincial Police video Travelling Alone gives many valuable safety tips. While the video is aimed at women, the information is useful for everyone. Contact your local OPP detachment for more information.

Here are some suggestions for coping with some common road emergencies:

If your brakes fail

Try pumping the brake pedal to temporarily restore hydraulic brake pressure. If this does not work, apply the parking brake gently but firmly while holding the release button. It is a good idea for new drivers to practise a parking brake emergency stop under controlled conditions with a qualified driving instructor. Total brake failure is very rare on modern vehicles. If your brakes do fail and you manage to stop, do not drive away. Call for help.

If your gas pedal sticks

First try to lift the pedal by slipping your foot under it. Do not reach down with your hands while the vehicle is moving. If this does not work, turn on your four-way emergency flashers, shift to neutral and stop as soon as you safely can, preferably off the road. Turn off the ignition and do not drive away. Call for help.

If your headlights go out

Check the switch immediately. If the lights stay out, turn on your four-way emergency flashers and bring your vehicle to a safe stop, off the road. Call for help. It is dangerous and illegal to drive at night without lights.

If you have trouble on a freeway

At the first sign of trouble, begin to pull over. Do not wait for your vehicle to stall on the freeway. Check your mirrors, put on your four-way emergency flashers, slow down, and pull over to the nearest shoulder as quickly as possible. Never stop in the driving lanes.

Be careful getting out of your vehicle. If possible, leave through the door away from traffic. If you need help, get back in the vehicle and put a "Call Police" sign in the side or back window. If you do not have a "Call Police" sign, tie a white cloth around the antenna. Do not raise the hood.

While you wait for help, stay in your vehicle with the doors locked. If someone stops to help, ask them to call the police or automobile club for you. If you have a cellular phone, call for help yourself.

XI. Dealing with emergencies

The Queen Elizabeth Way, the 400-series freeways, and many other high-speed roads are patrolled by the Ontario Provincial Police. Stay with your vehicle and help will arrive shortly.

If your wheels go off the pavement

Don't panic. Grip the steering wheel firmly. Take your foot off the gas pedal to slow down. Avoid heavy braking. When the vehicle is under control, steer toward the pavement. Be prepared to correct your steering and increase speed when your wheels are fully back on the pavement.

If a tire blows out

Blowouts can cause tremendous steering and wheel vibration, but don't be alarmed. Take your foot off the gas pedal to slow down and steer the vehicle firmly in the direction you want to go. Bring the vehicle to a stop off the road.

In a collision where someone is injured

St. John Ambulance recommends that all drivers carry a well-stocked first aid kit and know how to use it. Think about reading a book about first aid or sign up for a first aid course. It could mean the difference between life and death in a collision.

Every driver involved in a collision must stay at the scene or return to it immediately and give all possible assistance. If you are not personally involved in a collision, you should stop to offer help if police or other help has not arrived.

In a collision with injuries, possible fuel leaks or serious vehicle damage, stay calm and follow these steps:

- Call for help or have someone else call. By law, you must report any collision to the police when there are injuries or damage to vehicles or other property exceeding $700.
- Turn off all engines and turn on emergency flashers. Set up warning signals or flares or have someone warn approaching drivers.
- Do not let anyone smoke, light a match or put flares near any vehicle in case of a fuel leak. If any of the vehicles is on fire, get the people out and make sure everyone is well out of the way. If there is no danger of fire or explosion, leave injured people where they are until trained medical help arrives.
- If you are trained in first aid, treat injuries in the order of urgency, within the level of your training.

For example, clear the person's airway to restore breathing, give rescue breathing or stop bleeding by applying pressure with a clean cloth.

- If you are not trained in first aid, use common sense. Give the help you would hope to get if this happened to you. For example, people in collisions often go into shock. Cover the person with a jacket or blanket to reduce the effects of shock.
- Stay with injured people until help arrives.
- Disabled vehicles on the road may be a danger to you and other drivers. Do what you can to make sure everyone involved in a collision is kept safe.

In a collision where no one is injured

Follow these steps in a collision where there are no injuries:

1. If the vehicles are driveable, move them as far off the road as possible — this should not affect the police officer's investigation. This is especially important on busy or high-speed roads where it may be dangerous to leave vehicles in the driving lanes. If you cannot move the vehicles off the road, set up warning signals or flares far enough away to give other traffic time to slow down or stop.
2. Call police (provincial or local, depending on where the collision takes place). By law, you must report any collision to the police when there are injuries or damage to vehicles or property exceeding $700.
3. Give all possible help to police or anyone whose vehicle has been damaged. This includes giving police your name and address, the name and address of the registered owner of the vehicle, the vehicle plate and permit number and the liability insurance card.
4. Get the names, addresses and phone numbers of all witnesses.
5. If damage is less than $700, you are still required by law to exchange information with anyone whose vehicle has been damaged. However, the collision does not have to be reported to the police.

XII. Protecting the environment

Vehicles powered by gasoline and diesel give off air pollutants and gases such as oxides of carbon, nitrogen and sulphur, hydrocarbons and soot. These pollutants affect the quality of the air we breathe, our health, crop yields and even the global climate.

Hydrocarbons and oxides of nitrogen react in sunlight to form ground level ozone, better known as smog. Ozone is a major health hazard. Oxides of sulphur and nitrogen combine with water vapour to form acid rain, which damages our lakes, forests and crops.

Global warming is the result of too much carbon dioxide and other gases trapping heat in our atmosphere. Global warming could cause average temperatures to rise, causing droughts, crop failures, lower water levels and more frequent and severe storms.

A car gives off less carbon dioxide than a larger vehicle, such as an airplane, truck, bus or train, does. However, because so many people own cars and drive them so often, cars are responsible for half the carbon dioxide produced by all forms of transportation. Vehicles that carry large numbers of passengers, such as buses, produce less carbon dioxide per passenger than cars.

As a driver, you can help to protect the environment from the harmful effects of driving by following these suggestions:

1. Keep your vehicle well-tuned and make sure your tires are properly inflated. Have the pollution controls on your vehicle checked regularly.
2. Walk, cycle, carpool or take public transit instead of driving whenever possible.
3. Do not leave your engine running while your vehicle is parked.
4. If you are buying a new vehicle, buy the most efficient one you can. The less fuel a vehicle burns, the less pollution it creates.
5. Think about using fuels that are less harmful to the environment, such as propane, ethanol or natural gas.
6. If your vehicle has air conditioning, make sure it is not leaking refrigerant. Most car air conditioners use refrigerants that are harmful to the environment. These must be collected for recycling where you have your air conditioning system repaired.

10 WAYS YOU CAN HELP MAKE ONTARIO'S ROADS THE SAFEST IN NORTH AMERICA

1. Don't drink and drive. Don't drive when you're taking medication that will affect your driving.
2. Always wear your seat belt.
3. Obey the speed limits. Slow down when road and weather conditions are poor.
4. Don't take risks: don't cut people off in traffic, make sudden lane changes or run yellow lights.
5. Don't drive when you're tired, upset or sick.
6. If you're in doubt, let the other driver go first — yield the right-of-way.
7. Keep a two-second space between your vehicle and the one ahead. To check your distance: start counting when the vehicle ahead passes a fixed object, stop counting when your vehicle reaches the same spot.
8. Cut the distractions: don't overcrowd the vehicle or play loud music.
9. Always check your blind spot: look in your mirror and over your shoulder before you change lanes.
10. Check traffic in all directions before going into an intersection.

CHOOSING A DRIVING SCHOOL

As a new driver, choosing professional driving instruction may be the best way to put yourself safely in the driver's seat.

A driver training course or high school driver education program approved by the provincial government can teach you the skills and attitudes you need to be a safe and responsible driver. You may also be eligible to take your road test sooner and to save money on insurance premiums.

As well as teaching the basics, driver training emphasizes strategic driving techniques, risk perception and management, freeway driving, night driving and driving in adverse conditions. Most programs are designed for new drivers, but many schools also provide courses and services to upgrade your skills.

If you graduate from an approved program, the certificate you get will reduce the time you must spend at Level One by four months. It may also earn you savings on your car insurance.

Approved high school driver education programs offer in-class and in-car training after school for a fee. Courses are administered by the local school board, a principal or other high school authority. They are taught in high school classrooms by qualified instructors.

Approved driver training courses in Ontario must offer at least 25 hours of classroom training and 10 hours of behind-the-wheel training. Look for a program that offers high quality instruction and a comfortable learning environment. The school should also be equipped with up-to-date videotapes, overheads and other visual aids.

To help you choose the best driving school and course for you, use this checklist of features.

- Course information package
- Personalized program
- Classroom facilities
- Low student/teacher ratio
- Audio visual equipment
- In-vehicle topics covered
- Basic manoeuvres
- Strategic driving
- Risk perception and management
- Freeway driving
- Night driving
- Driving in adverse conditions
- Instructor qualifications and experience
- Regular instructor upgrading
- Student progress and evaluation reports
- Certificate of completion
- Minimum 25 classroom and 10 behind-the-wheel instruction hours
- Training materials
- Use of vehicle for road test
- Certification fee
- Registered educational institution
- Tuition receipts
- Testimonials
- Number of years in business
- Consumer protection insurance

TRAFFIC SIGNS AND LIGHTS

Traffic laws include the traffic signs and lights, pedestrian signals and pavement markings that tell drivers and other road users what they must do in certain situations. This chapter shows you what many of those signs, lights and markings look like and explains what they mean to drivers.

I. Signs

Traffic signs give you important information about the law, warn you about dangerous conditions and help you find your way. Signs use different symbols, colours and shapes for easy identification.

Here are some of the many signs you will see on Ontario roads:

A stop sign is eight-sided and has a red background with white letters. It means you must come to a complete stop. Stop at the stop line if it is marked on the pavement. If there is no stop line, stop at the crosswalk, marked or not. If there is no crosswalk, stop at the edge of the sidewalk. If there is no sidewalk, stop at the edge of the intersection. Wait until the way is clear before entering the intersection.

A school zone sign is five-sided and has a blue background with white symbols. It warns that you are coming to a school zone. Slow down, drive with extra caution, and watch for children.

I. Signs

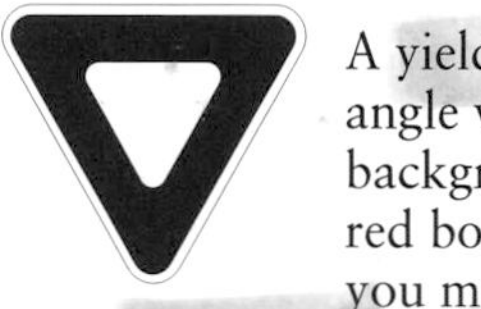

A yield sign is a triangle with a white background and a red border. It means you must let traffic in the intersection or close to it go first. Stop if necessary and go only when the way is clear.

A railway crossing sign is X-shaped with a white background and red outline. It warns that railway tracks cross the road. Watch for this sign. Slow down and look both ways for trains. Be prepared to stop.

There are four other kinds of signs: regulatory, warning, temporary conditions, and information and direction.

Regulatory signs

These signs give a direction that must be obeyed. They are usually rectangular or square with a white or black background and black, white or coloured letters.

A sign with a green circle means you may or must do the activity shown inside the ring. A red circle with a line through it means the activity shown is not allowed.

Here are some common regulatory signs:

This road is an official bicycle route. Watch for cyclists and be prepared to share the road with them.

You may park in the area between the signs during the times posted. (Used in pairs or groups.)

This lane is reserved for specific types of vehicles.

Snowmobiles may use this road.

Do not enter this road.

Do not turn left at the intersection.

Do not turn left during the times shown.

Do not stop in the area between the signs. (Used in pairs or groups.)

Do not drive through the intersection.

This parking space is only for vehicles displaying a valid Disabled Person Parking Permit.

Do not stop except to let passengers in or out of your vehicle. (Used in pairs or groups.)

Do not turn to go in the opposite direction. (U-turn)

No bicycles allowed on this road.

Do not park in the area between the signs. (Used in pairs or groups.)

Do not turn right when facing a red light at the intersection.

No pedestrians allowed on this road.

I. Signs

Keep to the right of the traffic island.

Speed limit changes ahead.

Do not pass on this road.

Slow traffic on multi-lane roads must keep right.

The speed limit in this zone is lower during school hours. Observe the speed limit shown when the yellow lights are flashing.

These signs, above the road or on the pavement before an intersection, tell drivers the direction they must travel. For example: the driver in lane one must turn left; the driver in lane two must turn left or go straight ahead; and the driver in lane three must turn right.

Traffic may travel in one direction only.

This is a pedestrian crossing or crossover. You must yield the right-of-way to pedestrians.

This sign, above the road or on the ground, means the lane is only for two-way left turns.

These signs mean lanes are only for specific types of vehicles, either all the time or during certain hours. Different symbols are used for the different types of vehicles. They include:

Keep to the right lane except when passing on two-lane sections where climbing lanes are provided.

This sign reserves curb area for picking up and dropping off passengers with disabilities.

buses
vehicles with three or more people
bicycles
taxis

I. Signs

Warning signs

These signs warn of dangerous or unusual conditions ahead such as a curve, turn, dip or sideroad. They are usually diamond-shaped and have a yellow background with black letters or symbols.

Here are some common warning signs:

Intersection ahead. The arrow shows which direction of traffic has the right-of-way.

Drivers on the sideroad at the intersection ahead don't have a clear view of traffic.

Posted under a curve warning, this sign shows the maximum safe speed for the curve.

Sharp bend or turn in the road ahead.

Narrow bridge ahead.

Pavement narrows ahead.

Chevron (arrowhead) signs are posted in groups to guide drivers around sharp curves in the road.

Road branching off ahead.

Slight bend or curve in the road ahead.

Winding road ahead.

The bridge ahead lifts or swings to let boats pass.

Paved surface ends ahead.

Bicycle crossing ahead.

Stop sign ahead. Slow down.

Share the road with oncoming traffic.

Pavement is slippery when wet. Slow down and drive with caution.

Hazard close to the edge of the road. The downward lines show the side on which you may safely pass.

The road ahead is split into two separate roads by a median. Keep to the right-hand road. Each road carries one-way traffic.

Right lane ends ahead. If you are in the right-hand lane you must merge safely with traffic in the lane to the left.

I. Signs

Traffic lights ahead. Slow down.

Snowmobiles cross this road.

Bump or uneven pavement on the road ahead. Slow down and keep control of your vehicle.

Steep hill ahead. You may need to use a lower gear.

Traffic travels in both directions on the same road ahead. Keep to the right.

Railway crossing ahead. Be alert for trains. This sign also shows the angle at which the railway tracks cross the road.

Two roads going in the same direction are about to join into one. Drivers on both are equally responsible for seeing that traffic merges smoothly and safely.

Underpass ahead. Take care if you are driving a tall vehicle. Sign shows how much room you have.

Sharp turn or bend in the road in the direction of the arrow. The checkerboard border warns of danger. Slow down; be careful.

Deer regularly cross this road; be alert for animals.

Truck entrance on the right side of the road ahead. If the sign shows the truck on the left, the entrance is on the left side of the road.

Shows maximum speed on ramp.

Watch for pedestrians and be prepared to share the road with them.

Watch for fallen rock and be prepared to avoid a collision.

There may be water flowing over the road.

This sign warns you that you are coming to a hidden school bus stop. Slow down, drive with extra caution, watch for children and for a school bus with flashing red lights.

These signs warn of a school crossing. Watch for children and follow the directions of the crossing guard or school safety patroller.

I. Signs

Temporary condition signs
These signs warn of unusual temporary conditions such as road work zones, diversions, detours, lane closures or traffic control people on the road. They are usually diamond-shaped with an orange background and black letters or symbols.

Here are some common temporary condition signs:

Construction work one kilometre ahead.

Road work ahead.

Survey crew working on the road ahead.

Traffic control person ahead. Drive slowly and watch for instructions.

You are entering a construction zone. Drive with extra caution and be prepared for a lower speed limit.

Temporary detour from normal traffic route.

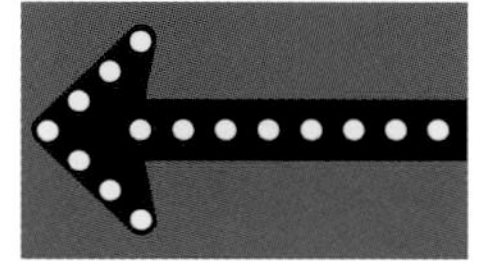

Flashing lights on the arrows show the direction to follow.

Information and direction signs

These signs tell you about distances and destinations. They are usually rectangular with a green background and white letters. Other signs with different colours guide you to facilities, services and attractions.

Here are some common information and direction signs:

Shows directions to nearby towns and cities.

Shows the distances in kilometres to towns and cities on the road.

Various exit signs are used on freeways. In urban areas, many exit ramps have more than one lane. Overhead and ground-mounted signs help drivers choose the correct lane to exit or stay on the freeway.

Advance signs use arrows to show which lanes lead off the freeway. Signs are also posted at the exit.

Emergency Response Signing

Some information signs include a numbering system along the bottom of the sign to assist emergency vehicles in determining an appropriate route.

Sometimes one or more lanes may lead off the freeway. The arrows matching the exit lanes are shown on the advance sign in a yellow box with the word 'exit' under them.

Freeway interchanges or exits have numbers that correspond to the distance from the beginning of the freeway. For example, interchange number 203 on Highway 401 is 203 kilometres from Windsor, where the freeway begins. Distances can be calculated by subtracting one interchange number from another.

I. Signs

The term 'VIA' is used to describe the roads that must be followed to reach a destination.

Shows route to passenger railway station.

Shows facilities available such as fuel, food, accommodation or camping.

Shows route to airport.

Shows types of fuel available:
D — diesel;
P — propane;
N — natural gas.

These signs change according to traffic conditions to give drivers current information on delays and lane closures ahead.

Shows route to ferry service.

Shows facilities that are accessible by wheelchair.

Other signs

Here are some other common signs:

The slow-moving vehicle sign is orange with a red border. Motor vehicles moving slower than 40 km/h must show this sign at the rear when driving on a road, unless they are only crossing it.

The new driver sign has a green background with black lettering. Placed in the back window of a vehicle, it tells other drivers that the driver is a novice.

Bilingual signs

Watch for these signs when driving in designated bilingual areas. Read the messages in the language you understand best. Bilingual messages may be together on the same sign or separate, with an English sign immediately followed by a French sign.

3

II. Traffic lights

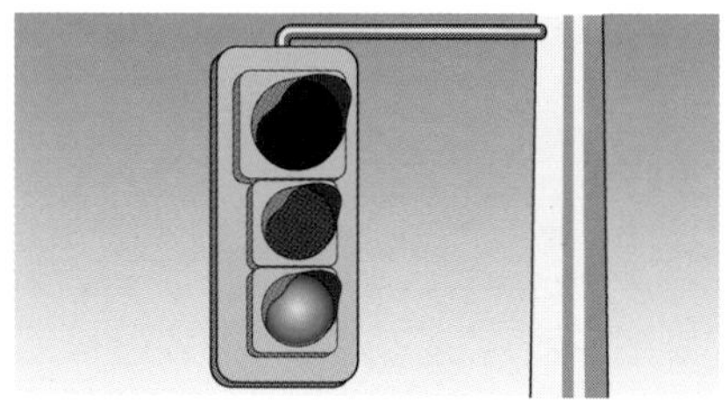

Traffic lights guide drivers and pedestrians through intersections and along roads. They tell road users when to stop and go, when and how to turn and when to drive with extra caution.

Green light

A green light means you may turn left, go straight or turn right after yielding to vehicles and pedestrians already in the intersection. When turning left or right you must yield the right-of-way to pedestrians crossing the intersection.

Yellow light

A yellow — or amber — light means the red light is about to appear. You must stop if you can do so safely; otherwise, go with caution.

Red light

A red light means you must stop. Bring your vehicle to a complete stop at the stop line if it is marked on the pavement. If there is no stop line, stop at the crosswalk, marked or not. If there is no crosswalk, stop at the edge of the sidewalk. If there is no sidewalk, stop at the edge of the intersection. Wait until the way is clear before entering the intersection.

Wait until the light changes to green and the intersection is clear before moving through it.

Unless a sign tells you not to, you may turn right on a red light only after coming to a complete stop and waiting until the way is clear. You may also turn left on a red light if you are moving from a one-way road into a one-way road, but you must come to a complete stop first and wait until the way is clear.

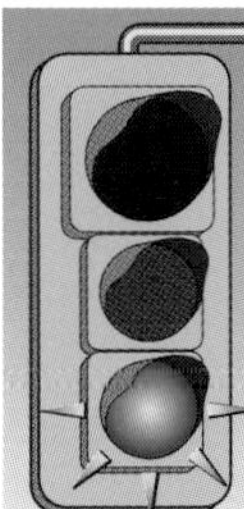

Lights and arrows to help turning vehicles

Flashing green lights and green arrows direct drivers who are turning.

Advance green light or arrow

When you face a flashing green light or a left-pointing green arrow and a green light, you may turn left, go straight ahead or turn right from the proper lane. This is called an advanced green light because oncoming traffic still faces a red light.

Pedestrians must not cross on a flashing green light unless a pedestrian signal tells them to.

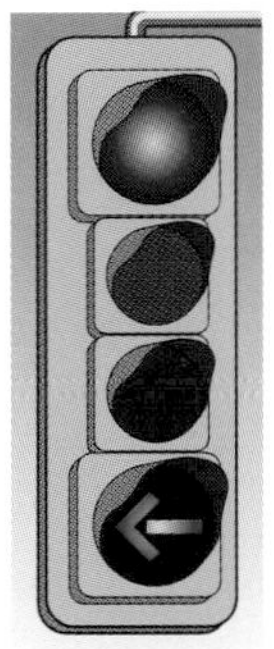

Simultaneous left turn

When a left-turn green arrow is shown with a red light, you may turn left from the left-turn lane. Vehicles turning left from the opposite direction may also be making left turns because they too face a left-turn green arrow.

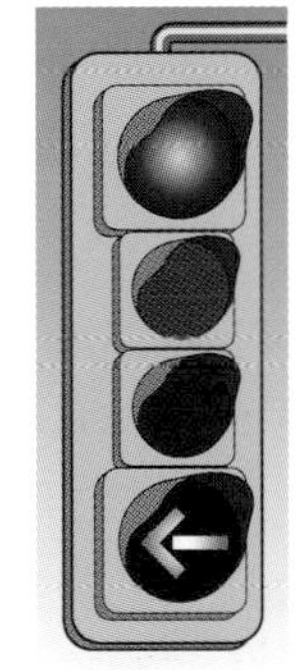

After the left-turn green arrow, a yellow arrow may appear. This means the green light is about to appear for traffic in both directions. Do not start your left turn. Stop if you can do so safely; otherwise, complete your turn with caution.

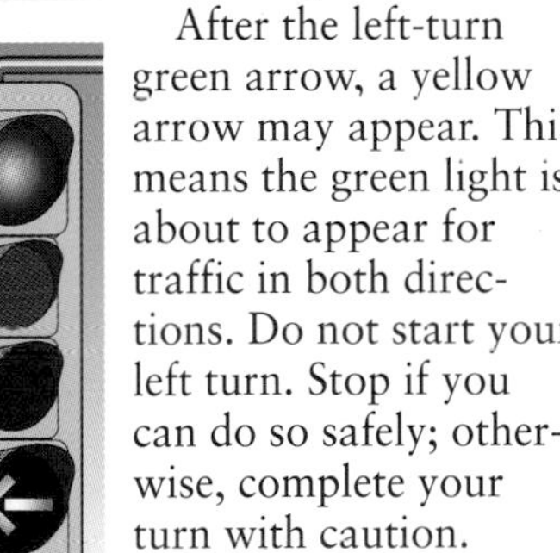

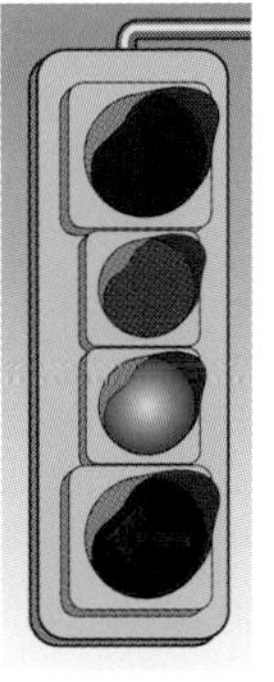

You can still turn left when the light is green, but only when the way is clear of traffic and pedestrians. If the light turns red when you are in the intersection, complete your turn when it is safe.

Pedestrians must not cross on a left-turn green arrow unless a pedestrian signal tells them to.

Transit Priority Signals

Traffic and pedestrians must yield to public transit vehicles at a transit priority signal. The round signal is on top of a regular traffic signal and shows a white vertical bar on a dark background. This allows transit vehicles to go through, turn right or left, while all conflicting traffic faces a red light.

II. Traffic lights

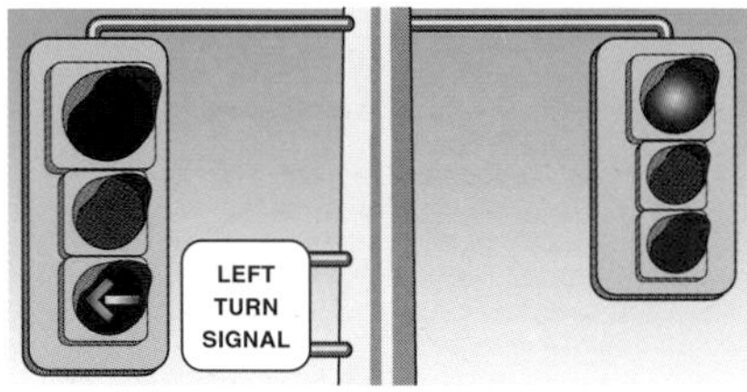

Fully protected left turn

Some intersections have separate traffic lights for left-turning traffic and for traffic going through the intersection or turning right.

When a left-turn green arrow appears for traffic in the left-turn lane, traffic going straight ahead or turning right will usually see a red light. You may turn left from the left-turn lane when you face a green arrow. Vehicles from the opposite direction may also be turning left.

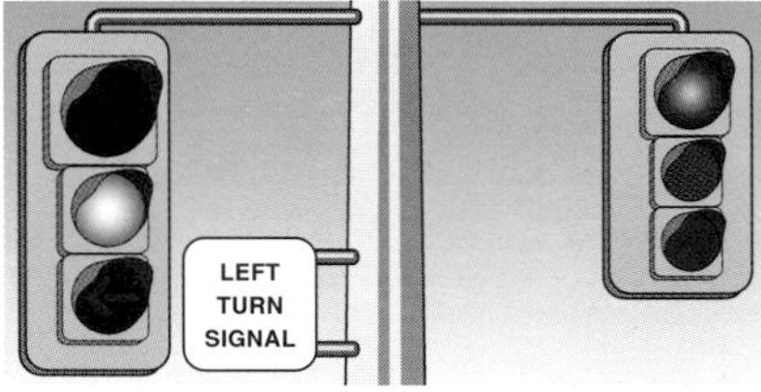

After the left-turn green arrow, a yellow light appears for left-turning vehicles only.

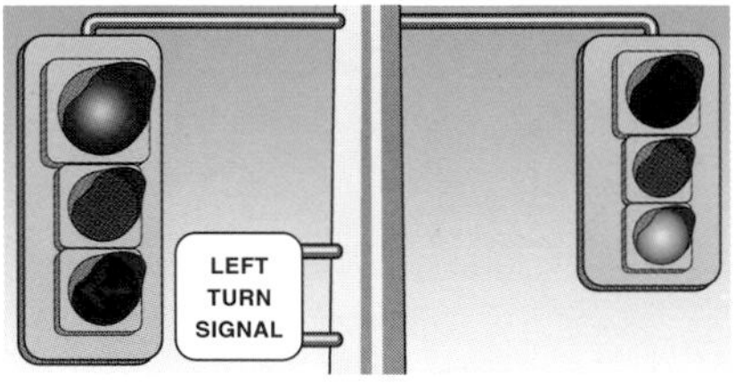

After the yellow light, a red light appears for left-turning vehicles only. Traffic going straight ahead or turning right will face a green light or green arrows pointing straight ahead and to the right.

In these intersections, you may not begin turning left after the green light appears for traffic going straight ahead or turning right. If the light turns yellow while you are in the intersection, complete your turn with caution.

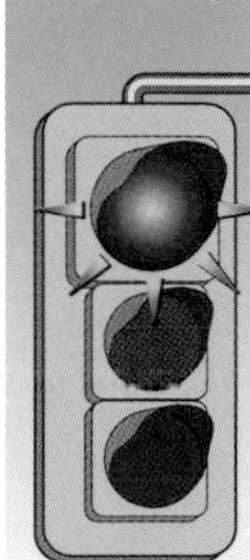

Flashing red light

You must come to a complete stop at a flashing red light. Move through the intersection only when it is safe.

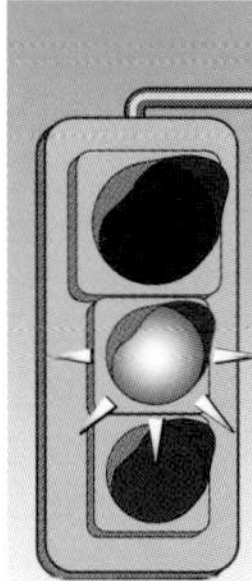

Flashing yellow light

A flashing yellow light means you should drive with caution when approaching and moving through the intersection.

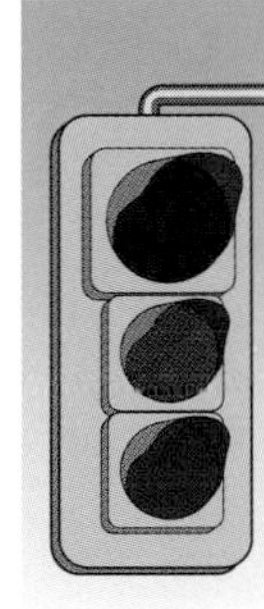
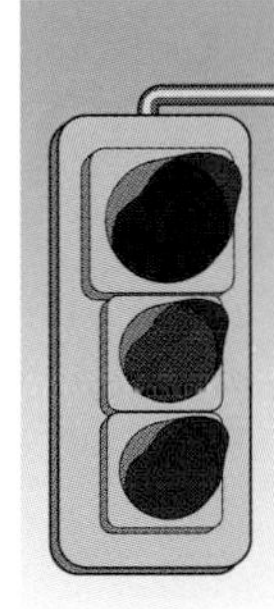

Blank traffic lights

During an electrical power loss, traffic lights at intersections will not work. Yield the right-of-way to vehicles in the intersection and to vehicles entering the intersection from your right. Go cautiously and use the intersection the same way you would use an intersection with all-way stop signs.

Traffic beacons

A traffic beacon is a single flashing light hung over an intersection or placed over signs or on obstacles in the road.

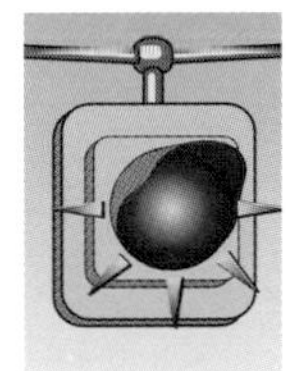

Flashing red beacon

A flashing red beacon above an intersection or stop sign means you must come to a complete stop. Move through the intersection only when it is safe to do so.

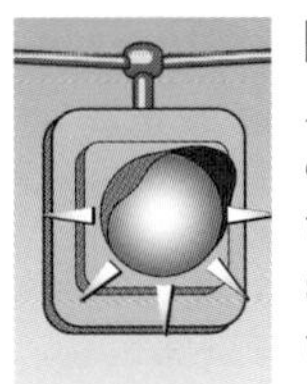

Flashing yellow beacon

A flashing yellow beacon above an intersection, above a warning sign or on an obstruction in the road, warns you to drive with caution.

III. Pedestrian signals

Pedestrian signals help pedestrians cross at intersections with traffic lights. The signal for pedestrians to walk is a white walking symbol. A flashing or steady orange hand symbol means pedestrians must not begin to cross.

A pedestrian facing a walk signal may cross the road in the direction of the signal. While crossing, pedestrians have the right-of-way over all vehicles.

Where there are pedestrian pushbuttons, a pedestrian must use the button to bring on the walk signal. Pedestrian signals give people more time to cross than regular traffic lights.

A pedestrian facing a flashing or steady hand symbol should not begin to cross the road. Pedestrians who have already begun to cross when the hand signal appears, should go as quickly as possible to a safe area. While they are crossing, pedestrians still have the right-of-way over vehicles.

At intersections with traffic lights where there are no pedestrian signals, pedestrians facing a green light may cross. Pedestrians may not cross on a flashing green light or a left-turn green arrow.

Intersection Pedestrian Signals

On a busy main road, an Intersection Pedestrian Signal helps people to cross the road safely by signalling traffic to stop. The Intersection Pedestrian Signal has one or more crosswalks, pedestrian walk/don't walk signals, push buttons for pedestrians, and traffic signal lights on the main road only. Stop signs control traffic on the smaller, less busy crossroad.

You must observe, obey the traffic rules, and use your safe driving skills to drive through these intersections. (See Driving Through Intersections on page 25.)

IV. Pavement markings

Pavement markings work with road signs and traffic lights to give you important information about the direction of traffic and where you may and may not travel. Pavement markings divide traffic lanes, show turning lanes, mark pedestrian crossings, indicate obstacles, and tell you when it is not safe to pass.

Diagram 3-1

Yellow lines separate traffic travelling in opposite directions. White lines separate traffic travelling in the same direction.

Diagram 3-2

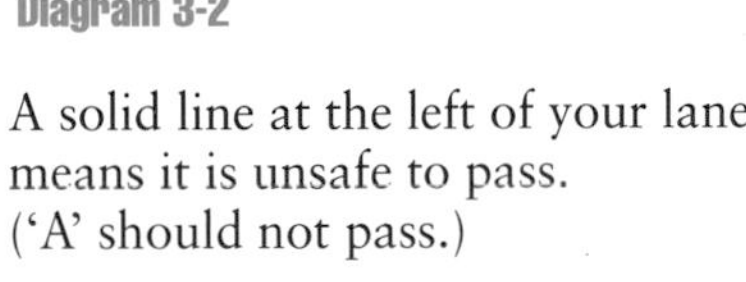

A solid line at the left of your lane means it is unsafe to pass.
('A' should not pass.)

IV. Pavement markings

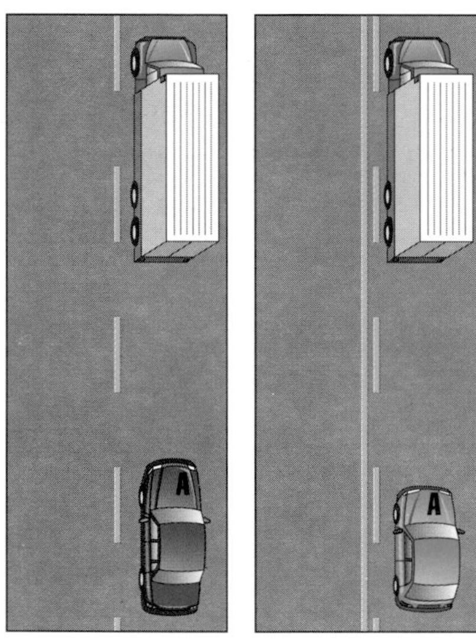

Diagram 3-3
A broken line at the left of your lane means you may pass if the way is clear. ('A' may pass if there are enough broken lines ahead to complete the pass safely.)

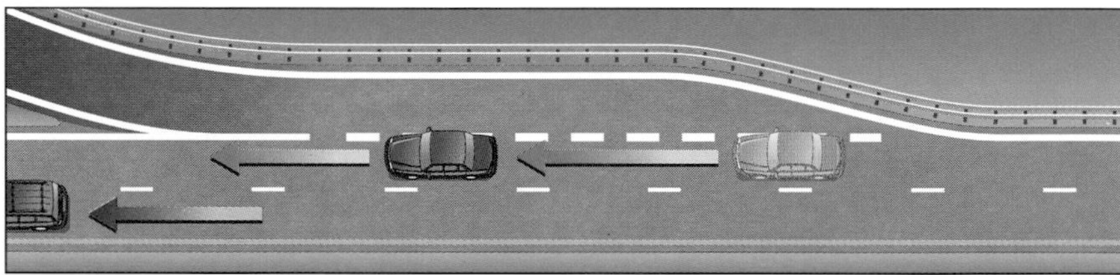

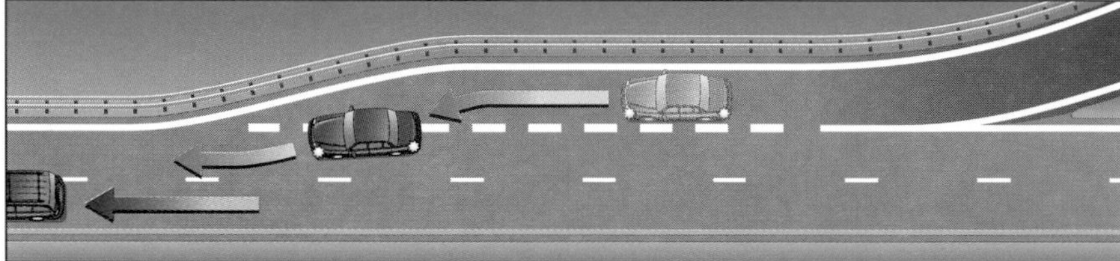

(Diagram 3-4: Above) Broken lines that are wider and closer together than regular broken lines are called continuity lines. When you see continuity lines on your left side, it means the lane you are in is ending or exiting and that you must change lanes if you want to continue in your current direction. Continuity lines on your right mean your lane will continue unaffected.

Diagram 3-5

A stop line is a single white line painted across the road at an intersection. It shows where you must stop. If there is no stop line marked on the road, stop at the crosswalk, marked or not. If there is no crosswalk, stop at the edge of the sidewalk. If there is no sidewalk, stop at the edge of the intersection.

Diagram 3-6

A crosswalk is marked by two parallel white lines painted across the road. However, crosswalks at intersections are not always marked. If there is no stop line, stop at the crosswalk, marked or not. If there is no crosswalk, stop at the edge of the sidewalk. If there is no sidewalk, stop at the edge of the intersection.

Diagram 3-7

A white arrow painted on a lane means you may move only in the direction of the arrow.

IV. Pavement markings

Diagram 3-8

A pedestrian crossing — or crossover — is marked by two white double parallel lines across the road with an X in each lane approaching it. Stop before the line and yield to pedestrians.

Diagram 3-9

Two solid lines painted on the pavement guide traffic away from fixed objects such as bridge piers or concrete islands. Yellow and black markings are also painted on the objects themselves as warnings.

KEEPING YOUR DRIVER'S LICENCE

Ontario is introducing a one-piece plastic driver's licence. The new card has a digitized photograph and signature of the driver and a magnetic information stripe. All drivers in Ontario should have the new licence by 2000. In the meantime, the two-piece licence with separate photo and licence card will still be used. Both the one-piece and the two-piece licences include your name, address and signature, date of birth, licence issue and expiry dates, and codes showing what class of vehicles you may drive and under what conditions.

You must carry your licence with you — one or two pieces, depending on the licence — whenever you drive.

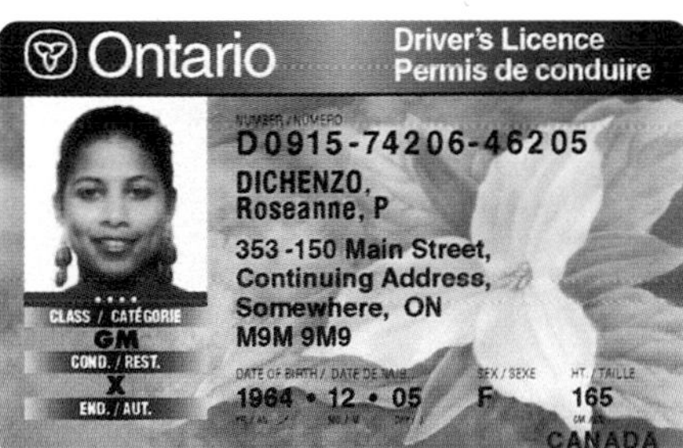

Diagram 4-1

KEEPING YOUR DRIVER'S LICENCE

Renewing your licence

All new Ontario licences will be one-piece licences. You will get a renewal application form in the mail. Take the form into any of the 360 Ministry of Transportation Driver and Vehicle Licence Issuing Offices, Driver Examination Centres and private issuing offices in the province. They are all equipped to take photographs. You will be asked to sign the form, show identification, pay a fee and have your photograph taken. You will get a temporary licence on the spot and your permanent one will be mailed to you. Carry it with you whenever you drive.

If you do not get a renewal application form in the mail when your licence is due for renewal, call the Ministry of Transportation. You are responsible for making sure you have a valid driver's licence. You can renew an expired car or motorcycle driver's licence within one year without taking any tests.

If you are a senior driver, 80 years or older, you must renew your driver's licence every two years. To do this, you must pass a vision test and a test of your knowledge of the rules of the road and traffic signs. You must also attend a group education session dealing with issues that face older drivers. For example, you will learn how the physical changes of aging can affect your driving and what you can do to reduce your risk of collisions as a result of those changes. You may also be asked to take a road test if there is a chance you may pose a safety risk. There is no charge for the tests and the group education session. You only have to pay the licence renewal fee.

Changing your name or address

You must tell the Ministry of Transportation within six days of changing your name or address.

REASON FOR NAME CHANGE	DOCUMENTATION REQUIRED
Marriage	Marriage certificate
Common-law alliance	Notarized affidavit of the fact
Adoption	Adoption papers
Under the Change of Name Act	Change of name certificate

You will need a new licence or licence card when you change your address. Take the change of information form to a Driver and Vehicle Licence Issuing Office, Driver Examination Centre or private issuing office or mail it to the Ministry of Transportation, P.O. Box 9200, Kingston, Ont. K7L 5K4. The ministry will send you a new licence or licence card. When you get it, destroy your old card and carry the new one with you whenever you drive.

When your name changes, you need a new licence. Take the documents you must show (see the chart on page 84) and your current licence to a Driver Examination Centre. A new photograph will be taken. You will get a temporary licence to use until your permanent licence is mailed to you. Carry it with you whenever you drive.

There is no charge for getting a new licence because you change your name or address.

The chart on page 84 shows the documents you will need to change the name on your driver's licence. If you don't have them, the ministry will look at your case individually.

Driver's licence laws

It is illegal to lend your licence or let someone else use it. It is also illegal to have an altered licence, to use another licence as your own, or to have more than one Ontario driver's licence.

The demerit point system

The demerit point system encourages drivers to improve their behaviour and protects people from drivers who abuse the privilege of driving. Drivers convicted of driving-related offenses have demerit points recorded on their records. (See the point system table on page 87.) Demerit points stay on your record for two years from the date of the offence. If you collect enough demerit points, you can lose your driver's licence.

New drivers

As a Level One or Level Two driver, you will have your licence suspended if you collect nine or more demerit points during a two-year period.

You will be sent a warning letter after two or more demerit points. At six points, you may have to go to an interview to discuss your record. If you don't go to the interview, your licence may be suspended. At nine points, your licence will be suspended for 60 days.

After the suspension, the number of points on your record will be reduced to four. Any extra points could again bring you to the interview level. If you reach nine points again, your licence can be suspended for six months.

Probationary drivers

Drivers who got their licences before April 1, 1994 must complete two years of probation before becoming fully licensed. Probationary drivers are automatically suspended if they collect six demerit points. You will be reminded of this by letter the first time you get demerit points. Your licence is suspended for 30 days from the time you hand it over to the Ministry of Transportation. You can lose your licence for up to two years if you fail to hand over your licence.

When the suspension is over, all points are removed from your driver's record and a new probationary period begins. You will stay on probation until you complete two one-year periods without being suspended. If your probationary period lasts more than three years you may be asked to complete a Level Two road test to become a fully licensed driver.

Fully licensed drivers

If you collect six demerit points, you will be told about your record and urged to improve your driving habits.

At nine points, you may have to go to an interview to discuss your record and give reasons why your licence should not be suspended. You may also have to complete a driver re-examination. If you fail this test, your licence can be cancelled. If you fail to attend an interview, or fail to give good reasons for keeping your licence, your licence may be suspended.

At 15 points, your licence will be suspended for 30 days from the date you hand over your licence to the Ministry of Transportation. You can lose your licence for up to two years if you fail to hand over your licence.

After the suspension, the number of points on your driver's record will be reduced to seven. Any extra points could again bring you to the interview level. If you reach 15 points again, your licence will be suspended for six months.

Table of offences

Here are the demerit point penalties for driving offences.

7 points

- Failing to remain at the scene of a collision

6 points

- Careless driving
- Racing
- Exceeding the speed limit by 50 km/h or more
- Failing to stop for a school bus

5 points

- Driver of bus failing to stop at unprotected railway crossing

4 points

- Exceeding the speed limit by 30 to 49 km/h
- Following too closely

3 points

- Exceeding the speed limit by 16 to 29 km/h
- Driving through, around or under a railway crossing barrier
- Failing to yield the right-of-way
- Failing to obey a stop sign, traffic light or railway crossing signal
- Failing to obey the directions of a police officer
- Driving the wrong way on a divided road
- Failing to report a collision to a police officer
- Improper driving where road is divided into lanes
- Crowding the driver's seat
- Going the wrong way on a one-way road
- Driving or operating a vehicle on a closed road
- Crossing a divided road where no proper crossing is provided

2 points

- Failing to lower headlight beam
- Improper opening of a vehicle door
- Prohibited turns
- Towing people — on toboggans, bicycles, skis, for example
- Failing to obey signs
- Failing to stop at a pedestrian crossing
- Failing to share the road
- Improper right turn
- Improper left turn
- Failing to signal
- Unnecessary slow driving
- Reversing on a divided high-speed road
- Driver failing to wear a seat belt
- Driver failing to ensure that a passenger less than 23 kg is buckled into seat belt or child safety seat
- Driver failing to ensure passenger under 16 years wearing seat belt

Other ways to lose your licence

You may also lose your licence for the following reasons:

Medical suspension

By law, all doctors must report the names and addresses of everyone 16 years or older who has a condition that may affect their ability to drive safely. Addiction to alcohol or drugs are conditions that affect your ability to drive. Doctors report this information to the Ministry of Transportation and it is not given to anyone else. Your driver's licence may be suspended until new medical evidence shows that the condition does not pose a safety risk.

Discretionary HTA suspensions

Your licence **may** be suspended:

- If you don't tell the truth:
  - in an application, declaration, affidavit or paper required by the Highway Traffic Act, its Regulations or the Ministry of Transportation.
  - about vehicle liability insurance.
- If you fail to insure your vehicle.
- If you are convicted of some driving offenses, included careless driving and driving 50 km/h or more over the speed limit.

Mandatory HTA suspensions

Your licence **will** be suspended:

- If you are convicted of failing to stop for a police officer and the court believes you wilfully avoided police during pursuit — that you tried to escape the police. (Your licence will be suspended for three years.)
- If you don't pay a traffic fine when ordered by the court.

Administrative suspension

Your licence will be suspended **immediately** for 90 days:

- If you fail or refuse to give a breath or blood sample when asked by police.
- If you have more than an .08 per cent blood alcohol level.

This suspension takes effect while you are still at the roadside or at the police station. It is an administrative suspension by the Registrar of Motor Vehicles and is separate from any criminal charges or prosecution which may also take place.

Your licence will be cancelled:

- If you fail a driver's re-examination.
- If you don't pay your licence renewal fee.

Criminal Code suspensions

A Criminal Code suspension is at least one year for the first time you are convicted of an offence; at least two years if you are convicted a second time within the next five years; and at least three years for any more convictions if they happen within five years. (These are called "subsequent" convictions.) The court can order a longer suspension if it believes that keeping you off the road will improve safety.

Your licence will be suspended if you are convicted of any of the following Criminal Code offences:

- Driving or having care and control of a vehicle while your ability is impaired by alcohol or drugs
- Refusing to submit to a breath test for alcohol
- Failing or refusing to provide a breath sample for roadside testing
- Driving or having care and control of a vehicle when you have more than an .08 per cent blood alcohol level
- Failing to remain at the scene of a collision to escape criminal or civil liability
- Dangerous driving
- Causing bodily harm by criminal negligence
- Causing death by criminal negligence

Driving under suspension

You may not drive, under any circumstances, when your licence is suspended. If you are convicted of driving while your licence is suspended for an HTA offence, you will have to pay a fine ($500 to $5,000 for a first offence; $1,000 to $5,000 for a subsequent offence) or spend six months in jail, or both. As well, your licence will be suspended for another six months beyond any other suspension.

There is a fine for driving when your licence is cancelled.

If you are found guilty of driving while your licence is suspended for a Criminal Code offence, you face an additional suspension (one year for a first offence; two years for a subsequent offence) under the HTA and up to two years in prison and three years licence suspension under the Criminal Code.

Other ways to lose your licence

Impaired driving

Impaired driving, which means driving when your ability is affected by alcohol or drugs, is a crime in Canada. If you are impaired, you can be convicted of several offences under the Criminal Code of Canada. Your vehicle does not even have to be moving; you can be charged if you are impaired behind the wheel, even if you have not started to drive.

Alcohol

Drinking and driving is a deadly combination.

All drivers, especially inexperienced drivers, must be able to concentrate on driving. That's why the graduated licensing system does not allow new drivers to drink any alcohol when they are going to drive.

Even one drink can reduce your ability to concentrate, to watch out for and react to things that happen suddenly when you are driving. With more alcohol in your blood, you could have trouble judging distances and your vision may become blurred. Factors like fatigue, your mood, and how long ago you ate and how much, can make a difference in how alcohol affects your driving ability.

The police have the right to stop any driver they suspect is impaired. They may also do roadside spot checks. When you are stopped by the police, you may be told to blow into a machine that tests your breath for alcohol — a roadside screening device. If you refuse, you will be charged under the Criminal Code. The police will also notify the Registrar of Motor Vehicles and your licence will be suspended immediately for 90 days.

If the reading on the machine shows you have been drinking, you may be taken to a police station for a breathalyser test. The breathalyser uses your breath to measure the amount of alcohol in your bloodstream and is expressed as a percentage.

If you cannot give a breath sample for some reason, the police officer

can ask you to let a doctor take a blood sample instead. If you are injured and cannot give your consent, a justice of the peace may authorize a doctor to take a blood sample.

The maximum legal blood alcohol concentration for fully licensed drivers is .08 per cent. Any more than .08 per cent is against the law.

If your reading is less than .08 per cent but .05 per cent or more, or if you register 'warn' on a roadside screening device, the police can suspend your licence for 12 hours. This keeps you from driving until your blood alcohol level drops. You must give your licence to the police officer on demand. The police will tell you when the 12-hour suspension will end and where to get your licence back. Meanwhile, if there is no one else available to drive and no safe place to park your vehicle, it will be towed at your expense.

If your blood alcohol concentration is more than .08 per cent, you will be charged under the Criminal Code. The police will also notify the Registrar of Motor Vehicles and your licence will be suspended immediately for 90 days. Even if your blood alcohol concentration is less than .08 per cent, you can still be charged with impaired driving under the Criminal Code.

Level One and Level Two drivers must have a blood alcohol level of zero when driving. New drivers caught drinking and driving will get a 30-day suspension for violating a condition of their Level One or Level Two licence. They can also be charged under the Criminal Code.

Drugs

Any drug that changes your mood or the way you see and feel about the world around you will affect the way you drive. The Criminal Code and HTA suspensions apply to drivers impaired by alcohol or drugs.

Illegal drugs such as marijuana and cocaine are not the only problem. Some drugs that your doctor may prescribe for you and some over-the-counter drugs can also impair your driving. Here are some points you should remember:

- If you use prescription medicines or get allergy shots, ask your doctor about side effects such as dizziness, blurred vision, nausea or drowsiness that could affect your driving.

Other ways to lose your licence

- Read the information on the package of any over-the-counter medicine you take. Any stimulant, diet pill, tranquillizer or sedative may affect your driving. Even allergy and cold remedies may have ingredients that could affect your driving.
- Drugs and alcohol together can have dangerous effects, even several days after you have taken the drug. Do not take a chance — ask your doctor or pharmacist.

Consider the consequences

Having your licence suspended is not the only cost of impaired driving. Depending on whether it is your first, second or subsequent offence, you can be fined, sent to jail for up to five years and prohibited from driving for up to three years.

For impaired driving that causes injury or death, the penalties are even more severe. You may lose your licence for up to 10 years if convicted. If you are convicted of impaired driving causing bodily harm, you may also be sentenced to up to 10 years in prison. Impaired driving causing death can carry a sentence of up to 14 years in prison.

If you have been drinking and are involved in a collision, your insurance company may not have to pay for damage to your vehicle. If you are injured in the collision, your medical and rehabilitation costs may not be covered.

If you drive for a living, a licence suspension could mean losing your job. And when you do get your licence back, you may find your insurance costs 50 to 100 per cent more for at least three years.

YOUR VEHICLE

All motor vehicles on Ontario roads must be registered, insured and maintained to meet certain basic safety standards. If you own a vehicle, you are responsible for making sure it meets the requirements. People who buy and sell vehicles also have certain responsibilities.

I. Maintaining your vehicle

It is illegal to drive a vehicle in dangerous condition. But maintaining your vehicle also makes sense from an economic point of view: it can mean better mileage and a better price when you sell your vehicle. Maintaining your vehicle also helps to protect the environment.

A police officer or Ministry of Transportation inspector can examine your vehicle, its equipment and any trailer attached to it, at any time. If the vehicle is found to be unsafe, it may be taken off the road until the problem is fixed. If you refuse to allow the examination, you can be fined up to $1,000. If the vehicle is then found to be unsafe, your licence plates can be taken away.

The following types of regular maintenance will help keep your vehicle fit and safe.

I. Maintaining your vehicle

Daily or weekly checks

- Keep your vehicle clean, inside and out. Keep seat belts clean to prevent dirt and moisture from damaging the mechanism.
- Check tire pressure. Properly inflated tires mean better mileage and safer driving. Also, check tires for damage or wear.
- Check that all lights are working.
- Check that windshield wipers are properly attached to wiper blades. If your wiper blades leave streaks on the window, replace them.
- Check under the hood when the engine is cold. Check that there is enough oil, water in the radiator, windshield washer fluid, brake fluid and battery fluid, if appropriate. Check all hoses for cracks or leaks and check fan belts for wear or slackness.

Diagram 5-1

Regular service

- Change oil and filter
- Change transmission fluid
- Change axle differential oil
- Check drive and axle shafts
- Check steering, brake and clutch reservoirs
- Check cooling system levels
- Check brake system
- Check front suspension, including alignment and condition of ball joints, steering rods, shock absorbers and springs
- Check engine adjustments — valve clearances, ignition timing, distributor and spark plugs
- Check carburettor or fuel injection system and air filter element
- Check headlight aim.

Winter maintenance

A well-maintained vehicle will generally start in all weather conditions. However, whenever possible, shelter your vehicle from direct contact with rain or snow when it is parked because even the best maintained vehicle can't run if the engine is soaked.

Carry emergency supplies. These should include a shovel, a bag of sand, booster cables, emergency flares or warning lights, blanket and chain for towing. Always carry extra windshield washer fluid in the winter and refill the container when necessary.

Cold weather puts extra strain on your vehicle's systems. With lights, heater, defroster and radio all working at once, batteries do not get a good charge at idle speed. If idling in traffic for long periods, shift to neutral and rev the engine gently. Have your battery checked and terminals cleaned at least twice during the winter.

Faulty exhaust systems are especially dangerous in the winter when drivers are more likely to drive with windows and vents closed. Have your exhaust checked if it sounds noisy or rattles.

Tires

The type of tires you have and the way they are made are critical for good traction, mileage and safety. Keep these points in mind when you buy or replace tires, and check your vehicle owner's manual or the tire manufacturer's guide for recommendations.

Tires must meet standards described in the Motor Vehicle Tire Safety Act.

- Replace tires when the tread is less than 1.5 millimetres deep or when tread wear indicators touch the road. Vehicles that weigh more than 4,500 kilograms must replace their front tires when tread is less than three millimetres deep.

I. Maintaining your vehicle

- Replace tires with bumps, bulges, knots, exposed cords, or tread and sidewall cuts deep enough to expose cords.
- Any tire on a vehicle must not be smaller than the vehicle manufacturer's specified minimum size. And it must not be so large that it touches the vehicle or affects its safe operation.
- Use similar tires on all four wheels. Some combinations are illegal, including: radial-ply tires on the front and bias-ply or belted bias-ply on the rear; a mix of 50 or 60 series tires on the front with any other mixture on the rear; and a combination of types or sizes on the same axle, unless the types and sizes are equivalent by industry standards. This does not apply to a single spare tire used in an emergency.
- The pressure of the spare tire should be the same as the pressure of the tire with the highest pressure.
- Any tire with the wording "not for highway use," "farm use only," "competition circuit only," "NHS," "TG," "SL" or any other words that mean the tire is not for use on the road must not be used on a vehicle that travels on roads.
- Although snow tires or all-weather tires are not required by law, they give the best traction for vehicles in winter. Install snow tires at least on the drive wheels. Four snow or all-weather tires are best for vehicles in snowbelt areas.
- Studded tires are illegal in Ontario.
- Scrap tires are a serious environmental concern. Proper tire maintenance will extend the life of a tire and delay its disposal. Some tips for longer wear: maintain the right air pressure; inspect tires for wear; rotate tires regularly; and practise good driving habits.

Diagram 5-2

II. Vehicle insurance and registration

Insurance

Ontario has compulsory automobile insurance. This means every vehicle registered in the province must be insured.

You must show proof that you have insurance coverage before you can register a vehicle or renew your registration. If you do not tell the truth about your insurance or if you show false documents, you can be fined $500 to $2,500. You may also lose your driver's licence for up to one year and have your vehicle taken away for up to three months.

You must insure all your vehicles for third party liability of at least $200,000. This covers you in the event that you injure or kill someone or damage someone's property. Collision insurance to cover damage to your own vehicle is a good idea but not required by law.

When driving your own vehicle or someone else's, you must carry the pink liability insurance card given to you by the insurance company for that particular vehicle. You must show this card when a police officer asks for it. If you do not, you can be fined up to $200.

Registration

Vehicle registration includes licence plates and a vehicle permit.

Licence plates in Ontario work on a plate-to-owner system. This means that vehicle licence plates move with the vehicle owner, not the vehicle. When you sell or change vehicles, you must remove your plates. If you do not intend to use them on another vehicle, you may return your plates to a Ministry of Transportation Driver and Vehicle Licence Issuing Office.

Your vehicle permit must have an accurate description of your vehicle. This means that if you change anything about your vehicle, such as the colour, you must report it at a Driver and Vehicle Licence Issuing Office within six days.

If you own a vehicle and you change your name or address, you must notify the Ministry of Transportation within six days. You can do this in person at a Driver and Vehicle Licence Issuing Office or by mail, using the change of information stub attached to your vehicle permit.

New residents

New Ontario residents have 30 days to register their vehicles. To get a vehicle permit and Ontario licence plates, go to a Driver and Vehicle Licence Issuing Office. You must bring along:

- A Safety Standards Certificate.
- Proof of insurance.
- A K-22 customs card if you have brought the vehicle in from another country.
- The vehicle permit, or ownership, from where you used to live.

III. Buying or selling a used vehicle

If you are selling a used vehicle privately in Ontario, you must buy a Used Vehicle Information Package. This applies to the private sale of any car, van, light truck, motor home or motorcycle. The package is available from any Ministry of Transportation Driver and Vehicle Licence Issuing Office or through the Ministry of Consumer and Commercial Relations.

The package, which the seller must show to potential buyers, has a description of the vehicle, its registration and lien history in Ontario, and the average wholesale and retail values for its model and year. It also includes information about retail sales tax.

As well as giving the buyer the Used Vehicle Information Package, sellers must remove their licence plates, sign the vehicle transfer portion of their vehicle permit and give it to the buyer. Sellers must keep the plate portion of the permit.

The buyer must take the package and the vehicle portion of the permit to a Driver and Vehicle Licence Issuing Office to register as the new owner within six days of the sale.

Before buyers can put their own plates on their new vehicle, they must have:

- their licence plates validated.
- the vehicle portion of the permit issued for the vehicle.
- their own licence plate number recorded on the plate portion of the vehicle permit.
- a valid Safety Standards Certificate.
- the minimum insurance required under the Compulsory Automobile Insurance Act.

Diagram 5-3

IV. Towing

Safety Standards Certificate

A Safety Standards Certificate is a document that certifies a vehicle's fitness. You can buy and register a vehicle without a safety certificate, but you cannot put your own plates on the vehicle or drive it without one. Any inspection station in Ontario licensed by the Ministry of Transportation can issue a Safety Standards Certificate, provided your vehicle passes an inspection. Many garages are licensed — look for a sign saying it is a Motor Vehicle Inspection Station.

A Safety Standards Certificate is valid for 36 days after the inspection. However, the certificate is not a guarantee or warranty that the vehicle will stay fit for any period.

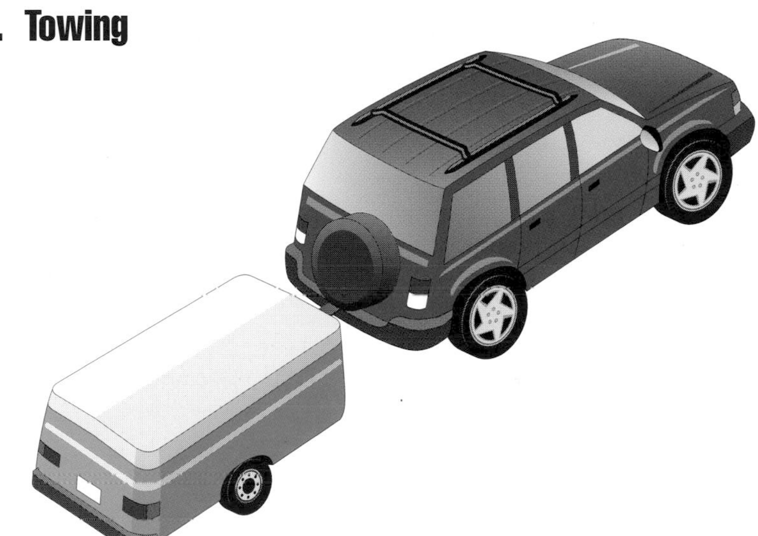

Towing a trailer

Follow these rules when towing trailers and similar vehicles:

- Unless it is a commercial vehicle, a vehicle may tow only one trailer at a time.
- Use two separate methods for attaching the trailer. For example, use a tow bar and a ball-attachment with safety chain. This does not apply to fifth-wheel attachments.
- It is against the law to carry people in a house trailer or boat trailer.
- The driver must make sure no one riding a bicycle, coaster, roller skates, skis, toboggan, sled or toy vehicle holds on to the vehicle.

IV. Towing

For more detailed information on towing trailers, including driving techniques and the special licensing and lighting requirements, consult the Official Off-Road Vehicles Handbook.

Towing disabled vehicles

If your vehicle breaks down, you should get help from a tow truck designed to tow vehicles. If you must use another vehicle to tow, use warning signals or emergency flashers and make sure you attach the vehicles securely. Someone must sit in the disabled vehicle and use the brakes to keep the tow cable tight. If the engine cannot run, don't tow vehicles that have power braking and steering. Without the engine, braking and steering is difficult and towing may lead to a collision.

Trying to start a disabled vehicle by towing is dangerous and could damage both vehicles.

THE LEVEL TWO ROAD TEST

Statistics show that new drivers of all ages are far more likely than experienced drivers to be involved in serious or fatal collisions.

To help new drivers develop better, safer driving habits, Ontario introduced graduated licensing in 1994 for all drivers applying for their first car or motorcycle licence. Graduated licensing lets you gain driving skills and experience gradually, in lower-risk environments. The two-step licensing system takes at least 20 months to complete and includes two road tests. Passing the Level Two (G2) road test gives you full Class G driving privileges.

While the Level One road test deals with basic driving skills, the Level Two road test deals with advanced knowledge and skills that are generally gained with driving experience. When you take the test, the examiner will give you directions. As you complete the driving tasks, the examiner will watch to make sure you successfully perform the actions associated with them.

To help you prepare, this chapter tells you the various tasks and actions that you will be expected to perform in your Level Two road test. This is only a guide. For more information on the driving tasks, you should review chapters 2 and 3. The book Road Worthy can also help.

I. Left and right turns

The approach

This driving task begins when the examiner tells you to make a left or right turn and ends at the point just before you enter the intersection. Make sure you take the following actions:

Traffic check Before slowing down, look all around you. Use your mirrors to check traffic behind you. If you change lanes, remember to check your blind spot by looking over your shoulder.

Lane Move into the far left or far right lane as soon as the way is clear.

Signal Turn on your signal before slowing down for the turn unless there are vehicles waiting to enter the road from sideroads or driveways between you and the intersection. Wait until you have passed these entrances so that drivers will not think you are turning before the intersection.

Speed Steadily reduce speed as you approach the turn. In a vehicle with manual transmission, you may downshift into a lower gear as you slow down. Do not coast with your foot on the clutch pedal.

Space While slowing down, keep at least a two- to three-second distance behind the vehicle in front of you.

If stopped

You will need to do this driving task if you cannot complete your turn without stopping, either because the way is not clear or you face a stop sign or red traffic light. Remember to follow these actions:

Stop Come to a complete stop. Do not let your vehicle roll forward or backward. When traffic conditions allow, move forward to check that the way is clear or to start the turn. If you have to stop after you have passed the stop line, do not back up.

Space When stopped behind another vehicle at an intersection, leave enough space to pull out and pass without having to back up. Leaving this space protects you in three ways: it lets you pull around the vehicle in front if it stalls; it helps prevent you from being pushed into the vehicle ahead if you are hit from behind; and it reduces the risk of collision if the vehicle ahead rolls backward or backs up.

Stop line If you are the first vehicle approaching an intersection with a red light or stop sign, stop behind the stop line if it is marked on the pavement. If there is no stop line, stop at the crosswalk, marked or not. If there is no crosswalk, stop at the edge of the sidewalk. If there is no sidewalk, stop at the edge of the intersection.

Wheels When waiting to make a left turn, keep your front wheels straight. With your wheels turned left, your vehicle could be pushed into oncoming traffic. When waiting to turn right, keep the wheels straight if there is a risk of being pushed into pedestrians crossing the intersection. At a large intersection with curved sidewalks where you are turning right, angle your vehicle to follow the curb so that no other vehicle can fit between you and the curb.

I. Left and right turns

Turning

This driving task involves your actions as you make the turn. Remember to do the following:

Traffic check If you are stopped, waiting for a green light or for the way to be clear, keep checking traffic all around you. Just before entering the intersection, look left, ahead and right to check that the way is clear. If there is any doubt about the right-of-way, try to make eye contact with nearby drivers or pedestrians. If it is possible for another vehicle to overtake you while you are turning, check your blind spot before starting to turn. You have not properly checked traffic if another vehicle or pedestrian has the right-of-way and must take action to avoid your vehicle.

Both hands Use both hands to turn the steering wheel throughout the turn. You are most at risk from other traffic when turning. Using both hands on the wheel gives you maximum steering control when you need it most. An exception to this is if you have a disability that prevents you from using both hands.

Gears In a vehicle with manual transmission, do not shift gears during the turn. If you need to, you may shift gears immediately after the vehicle is moving but before it is well into the turn. You may also shift gears in an intersection wider than four lanes if not doing so would slow down other traffic. Generally, not changing gears gives you more control over your vehicle when turning.

Speed Move ahead within four to five seconds after it is safe to start. Make the turn at a steady speed, increasing speed as you complete the turn. Drive slow enough to keep full control of your vehicle without slowing down other traffic.

Wide/short Turn into the corresponding lane on the intersecting road without going over any lane markings or curbs.

Completing the turn

This driving task completes the turn. It begins when you enter the intersecting road and ends when you return to normal traffic speed. Take the following actions:

Lane End your turn in the lane that corresponds to the lane you turned from. If you are turning left onto a multi-lane road, return to normal traffic speed and move into the curb lane when it is safe to do so. If you are turning right onto a road where the right lane is blocked with parked vehicles or cannot be used for other reasons, move directly to the next available lane.

Traffic check As you return to normal traffic speed, check your mirrors to become aware of the traffic situation on the new road.

Speed Return to normal traffic speed by accelerating smoothly to blend with the traffic around you. In light traffic, accelerate moderately. In heavier traffic, you may have to accelerate more quickly. In a vehicle with manual transmission, shift gears as you increase speed.

II. Stop intersection

The approach

This driving task is done at intersections where you must come to a stop. It begins at the point where you can see the intersection and ends just before you enter the intersection. Be sure to follow these actions:

Traffic check

Before slowing down, look all around you. Use your mirrors to check traffic behind you.

Speed

Steadily reduce speed as you approach the intersection. In a vehicle with manual transmission, you may downshift into a lower gear as you slow down. Do not coast with your foot on the clutch pedal.

Space

While slowing down, keep at least a two- to three-second distance behind the vehicle in front of you.

The stop

This driving task includes the actions you take while stopped and waiting to move through the intersection. Remember these points:

Stop Come to a complete stop. Do not let your vehicle roll forward or backward. When traffic conditions allow, move forward to check that the way is clear or start across the intersection. If you have to stop after you have passed the stop line, do not back up.

Space When stopped behind another vehicle at the intersection, leave enough space to pull out and pass without having to back up. Leaving this space protects you in three ways: it lets you pull around the vehicle in front if it stalls; it helps prevent you from being pushed into the vehicle ahead if you are hit from behind; and it reduces the risk of collision if the vehicle ahead rolls backward or backs up.

Stop line If you are the first vehicle approaching an intersection with a red light or stop sign, stop behind the stop line if it is marked on the pavement. If there is no stop line, stop at the crosswalk, marked or not. If there is no crosswalk, stop at the edge of the sidewalk. If there is no sidewalk, stop at the edge of the intersection.

II. Stop intersection

Driving through

This task includes the actions you take as you drive through the intersection and return to normal traffic speed. Make sure to follow these actions:

Traffic check If you are stopped, waiting for a green light or the way to be clear, keep checking traffic all around you. Just before entering the intersection, look left, ahead and right to check that the way is clear. If there is any doubt about the right-of-way, try to make eye contact with nearby drivers or pedestrians. You have not properly checked traffic if another vehicle or pedestrian has the right-of-way and must take action to avoid your vehicle.

Both hands Keep both hands on the steering wheel as you drive through the intersection. You are most at risk from other traffic when you are crossing the intersection. Using both hands on the wheel gives you maximum steering control when you need it most. An exception to this is if you have a disability that prevents you from using both hands.

Gears In a vehicle with manual transmission, do not shift gears crossing the intersection. If you need to, you may shift gears immediately after the vehicle is moving but before it is well into the intersection. You may also shift gears in an intersection wider than four lanes if not doing so would slow down other traffic. Generally, not changing gears gives you more control over your vehicle.

Traffic check As you return to normal traffic speed, check your mirrors to become aware of the traffic situation after you have gone through the intersection.

Speed

Move ahead within four to five seconds after it is safe to start. Return to normal traffic speed by accelerating smoothly to blend with the traffic around you. In light traffic, accelerate moderately. In heavier traffic, you may have to accelerate more quickly. In a vehicle with manual transmission, shift gears as you increase speed.

III. Through intersection

The approach

This driving task is done at intersections where you may not need to stop. It begins at the point where you can see the intersection and ends just before the entrance to the intersection. Remember to do the following:

Traffic check

As you approach the intersection, look left and right for traffic on the intersecting road. If you have to slow down for the intersection, check your mirrors for traffic behind you.

Speed

Keep at the same speed as you go through the intersection unless there is a chance traffic may cross the intersection in front of you. If so, slow down or hold your foot over the brake, ready to slow down or stop. Watch for pedestrians about to cross the intersection and vehicles edging into the intersection or approaching at higher speeds.

Space

Keep at least a two- to three-second distance behind the vehicle in front of you.

Driving through

This driving task includes your actions from the time you enter the intersection until you have crossed it and are returning to normal traffic speed. Remember these points:

Lane Do not go over lane markings or change lanes in the intersection. If your lane is blocked by a vehicle turning left or a vehicle edging into the intersection from the right, slow down or stop instead of pulling out to go around the vehicle.

Both hands Keep both hands on the steering wheel as you drive through the intersection. You are most at risk from other traffic when you are crossing the intersection. Using both hands on the wheel gives you maximum steering control when you need it most. An exception to this is if you have a disability that prevents you from using both hands.

Gears In a vehicle with manual transmission, do not shift gears crossing the intersection. If you need to, you may shift gears immediately after the vehicle is moving but before it is well into the intersection. You may also shift gears in an intersection wider than four lanes if not doing so would slow down other traffic. Generally, not changing gears gives you more control over your vehicle.

Traffic check If you slowed down for the intersection, check your mirrors again before returning to normal traffic speed.

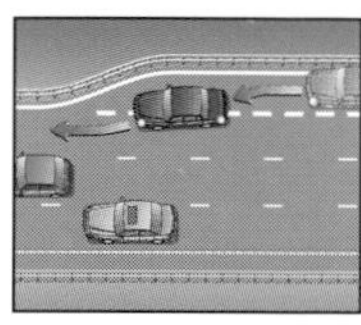

IV. Freeway

Entering

This driving task begins on the entrance ramp to a freeway and ends when you have reached the speed of the traffic on the freeway. Remember to do the following:

Traffic check

While on the ramp, as soon as you can see freeway traffic approaching from behind, check your mirrors and blind spot for a space to merge safely. At the same time, watch any vehicles in front of you on the ramp and keep back a safe distance. Continue to divide your attention between watching in front, checking your mirrors and looking over your shoulder to check your blind spot until you can merge safely with traffic.

Signal

If you have not done so already, turn on your signal as soon as traffic on the freeway is able to see your vehicle on the ramp.

Space

While on the ramp and merging with freeway traffic, keep at least a two- to three-second distance behind the vehicle in front of you. Time your merge so you do not move in beside another vehicle or into the blind spot of another vehicle. If traffic is heavy or moving at such a high speed that it is difficult to keep an ideal following distance, adjust your speed to get the best spacing possible. While on the ramp and in the acceleration lane, keep inside the lane markings.

Speed

On the curve of the entrance ramp, keep your speed slow enough so that objects and people inside your vehicle are not pushed from the force created by turning the curve. While in the acceleration lane, increase your speed to match that of freeway traffic. While merging, control your speed to blend smoothly with freeway traffic.

Merge Merge with freeway traffic in a smooth, gradual movement to the centre of the nearest freeway lane.

Cancel signal Turn off your signal as soon as you have merged with freeway traffic.

IV. Freeway

Driving along

This driving task checks your actions driving along the freeway but not merging, changing lanes or exiting. Be sure to remember the following points:

Traffic check While driving along, keep checking traffic all around you and look in your mirrors every five to 10 seconds.

Speed Avoid exceeding the speed limit or driving unreasonably slowly. Whenever possible, drive at a steady speed. Look ahead to where you are going to be in the next 12 to 15 seconds for dangerous situations or obstacles that you can avoid by changing your speed.

Space Always keep at least a two- to three-second distance behind the vehicle in front of you. If another vehicle follows too closely behind you, give yourself even more room in front or change lanes. Try to keep a space on both sides of your vehicle and try not to drive in the blind spots of other vehicles. Avoid driving behind large vehicles. Because of their size, they block your view of traffic more than other vehicles.

Exiting

This driving task begins when you are driving in the far right lane of the freeway and can see the exit you want to take. It ends when you reach the end of the exit ramp. Remember to do the following:

Traffic check Before moving into the exit lane, look left and right and check your mirrors. If there is a lane of traffic on your right, such as an acceleration lane from an entrance ramp, or a paved shoulder, remember also to check your right blind spot.

Signal Turn on your signal before you reach the exit lane.

Exit lane Enter the exit lane at the beginning of the lane with a smooth, gradual movement. Stay inside the lane markings. If there are two or more exit lanes, do not cross solid lines on the pavement to change lanes.

Speed Do not slow down before you are completely in the exit lane. Once you are in the lane, slow gradually without causing traffic to pile up behind you. On the curve of the exit ramp, keep your speed slow enough so that objects and people inside your vehicle are not pushed from the force created by turning the curve. In a vehicle with manual transmission, downshift as you reduce speed.

Space Keep at least a two-to three-second distance behind the vehicle in front of you.

Cancel signal Turn off your signal once you are on the exit ramp.

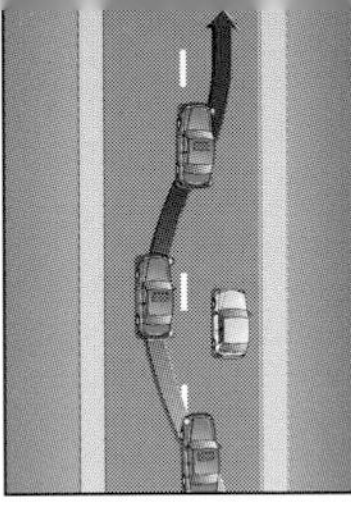

V. Lane change

This driving task begins as you look for a space to change lanes and ends when you have completed the lane change. Remember to follow these actions:

Traffic check

While waiting to change lanes safely, look all around you. Divide your attention between watching in front, watching the mirrors, and checking your blind spot. If there is another lane beside the one you are moving into, check traffic in that lane to avoid colliding with a vehicle moving into the lane at the same time as you do.

Signal

Turn on your signal when there is enough space for you to change lanes. After signalling, check your blind spot one more time before starting to move into the other lane. Your signal should be on soon enough to give traffic behind you time to react to the signal. If traffic in the lane you are moving into is heavy, you may turn on your signal before there is enough space to change lanes. This will let traffic behind you know that you are looking for a space to change lanes.

Space

Keep at least a two- to three-second distance behind the vehicle in front of you. If there is another lane beside the one you are moving into, be careful not to move in beside another vehicle or into the blind spot of another vehicle.

Speed

Adjust your speed to match the speed of traffic in the new lane.

Change

Change lanes with a smooth, gradual movement into the centre of the new lane.

Both hands

Keep both hands on the steering wheel as you change lanes. Using both hands on the wheel gives you maximum steering control. An exception to this is if you have a disability that prevents you from using both hands.

Cancel signal

Turn off your signal as soon as you have changed lanes.

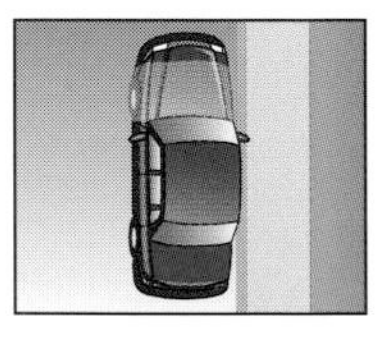

VI. Roadside stop

The approach

This driving task begins when the examiner tells you to stop and ends once you have come to a stop. Make sure you take these actions:

Traffic check Before slowing down, check your mirrors for traffic behind you. If there is a chance of traffic or pedestrians overtaking you on the right, check your right blind spot just before pulling over.

Signal Turn on your signal before slowing down unless there are vehicles waiting to enter the road from sideroads or driveways between you and the point where you intend to stop. Wait until you have passed these entrances so that drivers will not think you are turning before the stopping point.

Speed Steadily reduce speed as you approach the stop. In a vehicle with manual transmission, you may downshift into a lower gear as you slow down. Do not coast with your foot on the clutch pedal.

Position Stop parallel to the curb and not more than about 30 centimetres away from it. If there is no curb, stop as far as possible off the travelled part of the road. Do not stop where you will block an entrance or other traffic.

The stop

This driving task includes the actions you take after stopping. Remember to do the following:

Signal Turn off your signal and turn on your four-way flashers.

Park Put the gear selector into park, or shift into neutral if your vehicle has a manual transmission. Set the parking brake and turn off the vehicle. Take your feet off the pedals. Make sure the vehicle does not roll forward or backward after stopping.

VI. Roadside stop

Resume

This driving task begins when the examiner tells you to move back onto the road and ends when you have returned to normal traffic speed. Take the following actions:

Start Turn on the engine. Release the parking brake and select the correct gear to move back onto the road.

Signal Turn off your four-way flashers and turn on your left turn signal.

Traffic check Just before pulling away from the stop, check your mirrors and your left blind spot.

Speed Return to normal traffic speed by accelerating smoothly to blend with the traffic around you. In light traffic, accelerate moderately. In heavier traffic, you may have to accelerate more quickly. In a vehicle with manual transmission, shift gears as you increase speed.

Cancel signal Turn off your signal as soon as you are back on the road.

VII. Curve

This driving task begins when the curve comes into sight and ends when you have gone completely around it. Follow these actions:

Speed

As you approach the curve, try to determine the safe speed for the curve. To do this, look for clues such as a sign that shows the safe speed, the shape of the curve and the type of road you are driving on. Slow down to the safe speed for the curve by the time you are 30 metres into it. In a blind curve where you cannot see all the way around it, drive more slowly in case oncoming traffic wanders into your lane or the curve is tighter than you expected. **Slow down before the start of the curve to avoid braking in the curve.** While in the curve, keep your speed steady and slow enough so that objects and people inside your vehicle are not pushed from the force created by turning on the curve. Near the end of the curve, begin accelerating to return to normal speed. In a vehicle with manual transmission, do not shift gears in the curve. Not changing gears gives you more control over your vehicle and reduces the risk of your wheels locking while downshifting.

Lane

As you enter the curve, look as far around it as possible. This helps you stay in a smooth line and centred in the lane throughout the curve. If you look only at the road directly in front of you, you are likely to wander back and forth across the lane, forcing you to constantly correct your steering.

VIII. Business section

This driving task is done on straight sections of road where a number of businesses are located. Be sure to do the following actions:

Traffic check

In a business area, there are many places other than intersections where vehicles or pedestrians are likely to enter the road. These include entrances to businesses, institutions and construction sites, as well as pedestrian and railway crossings. At all these locations, look left and right to check for vehicles or pedestrians about to enter the road.

Mirror check

While driving along, check your mirrors every five to 10 seconds. Check your mirrors more often in heavy traffic or where vehicles are moving at different speeds.

Lane

Drive in the safest lane for through traffic. This is usually the curb lane. However, if the curb lane is blocked by traffic or there are many curbside hazards, the centre lane may be a safer choice. Keep to the centre of the lane and within the lane markings. Look ahead to where you will be in the next 12 to 15 seconds for dangerous situations or obstacles that you can avoid by changing lanes.

Speed

Avoid exceeding the speed limit or driving unreasonably slowly. Whenever possible, drive at a steady speed. Look ahead to where you will be in the next 12 to 15 seconds for dangerous situations or obstacles that you can avoid by changing your speed.

Space

Keep at least a two- to three-second distance behind the vehicle in front of you. Increase the distance if another vehicle follows too closely behind you. On a multi-lane road, try to keep a space on both sides of your vehicle and try not to drive in the blind spots of other vehicles. In slow traffic, avoid driving behind large vehicles that block your view of traffic ahead of you. When you stop behind another vehicle, leave enough space to see its rear wheels or to pull around it without having to back up.

IX. Residential section

This driving task is done on straight sections of residential or rural road. Remember these points:

Traffic check On a residential road, watch out for entrances to schools, pedestrian crossings, driveways, sidewalks and any other locations where there might be traffic hazards. On a rural road, watch for entrances to residences, farms, businesses and industrial sites. At all these locations, look left and right to check for vehicles or pedestrians about to enter the road.

Mirror check While driving along, check your mirrors every five to 10 seconds. Check your mirrors more often in heavy traffic or where vehicles are moving at different speeds.

Lane Keep to the centre of the lane. If there are no lane markings, keep to the centre of the travelled part of the road, away from parked vehicles or pedestrians. Where you cannot see far ahead on the road because of a curve or a hill, move right to avoid colliding with an oncoming vehicle that is over the centre line. Look ahead to where you will be in the next 12 to 15 seconds for dangerous situations or obstacles that you can avoid by changing lanes.

Speed Avoid exceeding the speed limit or driving unreasonably slowly. Whenever possible, drive at a steady speed. Look ahead to where you will be in the next 12 to 15 seconds for dangerous situations or obstacles that you can avoid by changing your speed.

Space

Keep at least a two- to three-second distance behind the vehicle in front of you. Increase the distance if another vehicle follows too closely behind you. In slow traffic, avoid driving behind large vehicles that block your view of traffic ahead. When you stop behind another vehicle, leave enough space to see its rear wheels or to pull around it without having to back up.

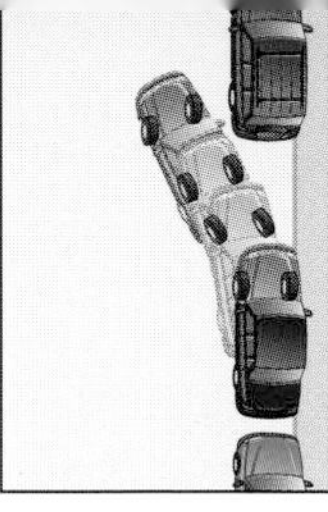

X. Parallel park

The approach

This driving task begins when the examiner tells you to park and ends when you have come to a stop, ready to back into the parking space. Remember these points:

Traffic check Before slowing down, check your mirror for traffic behind you. Before pulling into position to back up, check your blind spot.

Signal Turn on your signal before slowing down unless there are vehicles waiting to enter the road from sideroads or driveways between you and your stopping point. Wait until you have passed these entrances so that drivers will not think you are turning before your parallel parking position.

Speed Steadily reduce speed. In a vehicle with manual transmission, you may downshift into a lower gear as you slow down. Do not coast with your foot on the clutch pedal.

Stop Stop beside – or parallel to – the parked vehicle (real or imaginary) in front of the empty parking space. Leave at least 60 centimetres between your vehicle and the parked vehicle. Stop when your vehicle is completely in front of the empty parking space.

Park

This driving task includes the actions you take to park in a parallel parking space. Remember to do the following:

Traffic check Before backing up, look all around the vehicle and check your mirrors and both blind spots. Do not start reversing until the way is clear or traffic has stopped to let you park.

Back up Begin reversing into the space, turning the steering wheel towards the curb. When your vehicle is about halfway into the space, steer to bring your vehicle in line with the curb. Once you are in the parking space, move forward or backward to fit within the pavement markings or to allow room for the vehicle in front or behind you to pull out. Do not hit the curb or touch another vehicle while entering your parking space. Where there is no curb, park off the travelled part of the road.

Park Put the gear selector in park, or shift into neutral if your vehicle has a manual transmission, and set the parking brake. Turn off the engine. When parking on a hill, turn your wheels to keep your vehicle from rolling.

X. Parallel park

Resume

This driving task begins when the examiner tells you to move from the parking space and ends when you have returned to normal traffic speed. Remember these points:

Start Turn on the engine. Release the parking brake and select the correct gear to move back onto the road.

Signal Turn on your signal.

Traffic check Just before pulling out of the parking spot, check your mirrors and your blind spot.

Speed Return to normal traffic speed by accelerating smoothly to blend with the traffic around you. In light traffic, accelerate moderately. In heavier traffic, you may have to accelerate more quickly. In a vehicle with manual transmission, shift gears as you increase speed.

Cancel signal Turn off your signal after you leave the parking space.

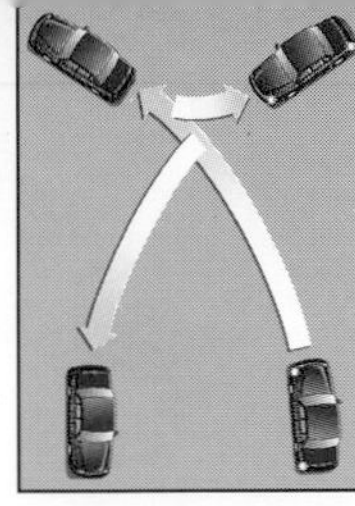

XI. Three-point turn

The approach

This driving task begins when the examiner tells you to stop and turn your vehicle around. It ends when you have almost stopped, ready to start the turn. Be sure to do the following:

Traffic check Before slowing down, check traffic in front and behind you. If necessary, check your blind spot before pulling over to the right side of the road to stop.

Signal Turn on your signal before slowing down unless there are vehicles waiting to enter the road from sideroads or driveways between you and your stopping point. Wait until you have passed these entrances so that drivers will not think you are turning.

Speed Steadily reduce speed. In a vehicle with manual transmission, you may downshift into a lower gear as you slow down. Do not coast with your foot on the clutch pedal.

Position Stop so you are parallel to the curb and not more than 30 centimetres away. Where there is no curb, stop as far as possible off the travelled part of the road. Do not stop where you will block an entrance or other traffic.

XI. Three-point turn

Turn around

This driving task includes the actions you take to turn around and ends when you are ready to drive away in the opposite direction. Remember these points:

Traffic check — Check your mirrors and your blind spot just before starting the turn. Wait until the way is clear or traffic has stopped to let you turn. Each time you stop while turning, check traffic in both directions.

Signal — Turn on your left signal before starting to turn.

Turn around — With the steering wheel turned sharply left, move slowly and smoothly across the road. When you have reached the far left side of the road, stop and put your vehicle in reverse. With the steering wheel turned sharply right, reverse so the vehicle is facing in the new direction. Stop and shift into forward gear to move ahead. Use the whole road to make your turn, reversing only once. Do not reverse over the edge or shoulder of the road or into the curb.

Resume

This driving task begins when you are turned around, ready to move ahead and ends when you have returned to normal traffic speed. Make sure you take these actions:

Traffic check Check your mirrors before increasing speed.

Speed Return to normal traffic speed by accelerating smoothly to blend with the traffic around you. In light traffic, accelerate moderately. In heavier traffic, you may have to accelerate more quickly. In a vehicle with manual transmission, shift gears as you increase speed.

Road Worthy

Road Worthy is a comprehensive guide to safe driving for new and experienced drivers.

It includes the rules of the road; skills for driving on any road, driving at night and in bad weather; basic vehicle maintenance; jump starting a vehicle; and changing a flat tire.

The text is clear and easy to understand, with many helpful diagrams and photographs.

Road Worthy is used in high school driver education classes in Ontario and by many commercial driving schools.

This hard-cover book with 168 pages of information will help you maintain your safe driving skills and enhance your driving enjoyment long after you pass your final road test.

(Available for purchase by calling Publications Ontario at (416) 326-5300 or 1 800 668-9938. Or visit us at our website at publications.gov.on.ca)

Diagram 5-4

INDEX

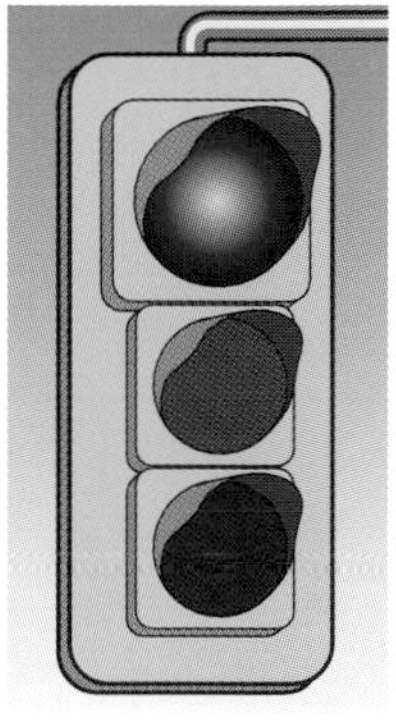

STOP! Did you know there are other books in the official driver information series?

Now you can purchase copies of this official handbook and five others from a retail store, a Driver Examination Office or a Vehicle Licence Issuing Office near you—or you can order them directly from the distributor.

Distribution: **General Publishing Co. Limited**
325 Humber College Blvd., Etobicoke, Ontario M9W 7C3
or by calling (416) 213-1919 ext. 199 or 1-800-387-0141 Fax (416) 213-1917

Prepayment required by cheque or credit card — VISA or Mastercard

QUANTITY				TOTAL
______	ISBN 0-7778-6141-0	The Official Driver's Handbook	$ 7.95	______
______	ISBN 0-7778-6143-7	The Official Motorcycle Handbook	$ 7.95	______
______	ISBN 0-7778-4456-7	The Official Off-Road Vehicles Handbook	$ 4.95	______
______	ISBN 0-7778-4454-0	The Official Truck Handbook	$ 7.95	______
______	ISBN 0-7778-4452-4	The Official Bus Handbook	$ 7.95	______
______	ISBN 0-7778-4450-8	The Official Air Brake Handbook	$ 12.95	______
			Sub-Total	______
			Plus 12%	______
			TOTAL	______

All prices are subject to 7% G.S.T. and 5% Shipping Costs. Please add 12% to your total purchase to cover G.S.T. and shipping cost.

Payment by cheque ☐ VISA ☐ Mastercard ☐

Credit Card No. ______________________ Expiry Date __________

Signature of Card Holder ______________________________

SHIP TO (PLEASE PRINT):

Name: ______________________________

Address: ______________________________

Town/City: ______________________________

Province: ______________ Postal Code: __________

ONTARIO TRANSPORTATION MAP Series—including the Official Road Map of Ontario

Get a more detailed look at specific areas of Southern Ontario with this series of eight maps, scaled at 1:250,000. You'll find enlargements of major city centres, highways, townships, municipal roads including loose surface and seasonal roads, railways, airports, parks, O.P.P. detachments, hospitals, tourist attractions and service centres within each region.

Or pick up the Official Road Map of Ontario, which shows all of Ontario's highways and major roads.

Purchase your maps now at retail outlets across Ontario, or order them directly from the distributor.

General Publishing Co. Limited
325 Humber College Blvd., Etobicoke, Ontario M9W 7C3 Telephone (416) 213-1919 ext. 199
OR 1-800-387-0141 Fax (416) 213-1917

Prepayment required by cheque or credit card VISA or Mastercard.

QUANTITY				TOTAL
________	Map #1	Southwestern Ontario	$ 7.00	________
________	Map #2	Lake Huron - Georgian Bay Area	$ 7.00	________
________	Map #3	Manitoulin Island	$ 7.00	________
________	Map #4	Central Ontario	$ 7.00	________
________	Map #5	South Central Ontario	$ 7.00	________
________	Map #6	Upper Ottawa Valley	$ 7.00	________
________	Map #7	Eastern Lake Ontario	$ 7.00	________
________	Map #8	Eastern Ontario	$ 7.00	________
________	Complete Set of 8 (for the price of seven)		$ 49.00	________
________	Official Road Map of Ontario		$ 2.95	________
			Sub-Total	________
			Plus 20%	________
			TOTAL	________

All prices are subject to G.S.T., P.S.T. and shipping costs. Please add 20% to your total purchase to cover taxes and shipping costs.

Payment by cheque ☐ VISA ☐ Mastercard ☐

Credit Card No. ____________________ Expiry Date __________

Signature of Card Holder ______________________________

SHIP TO (PLEASE PRINT):

Name: ______________________________

Address: ______________________________

Town/City: ______________________________

Province: ____________________ Postal Code: __________

EXPRESS YOURSELF!
with graphic licence plates for as low as $52.10
To order, and for more information, visit your local
Driver and Vehicle Licence Office
or ServiceOntario Kiosk
or call
1-800-AUTO-PL8 (1-800-288-6758)
Gift certificates available
© MLBP 1996 © NHL ENTERPRISES INC. 1996
© 1996 NBA Properties © CFL Properties
© Scouts Canada © Wilfrid Laurier University
© Ontario Lacrosse Association © RAC Inc.
© OFSC © Queens University © Shriners International
Queen's University
Road Safety
It starts with you
RAC
Tiger-Cats
Lacrosse
Scouts Canada
Toronto Blue Jays
Toronto Maple Leafs
Raptors
Ontario
Yours to Discover

Other Official Handbooks for You

Copies of this handbook and others may be purchased from a retail store near you, from a Driver Examination Office, from a Vehicle Licence Issuing Office or from the distributor.

Distribution:

General Publishing Co. Limited
325 Humber College Blvd.,
Etobicoke, Ontario
M9W 7C3

or by calling
(416) 213-1919 ext. 199
or 1 (800) 387-0141

Prepayment required by cheque or credit card — VISA or Mastercard

All prices are subject to 7% G.S.T. and 5% Shipping Costs. Please add 12% to your total purchase to cover G.S.T. and shipping cost.